Digital Design Essentials

Digital Design Essentials

100 Ways to Design Better
Desktop, Web, and
Mobile Interfaces

Raj Lal

Rockport Publishers
100 Cummings Center, Suite 406L
Beverly, MA 01915

rockpub.com • rockpaperink.com

First published in the United States of America in 2013 by
Rockport Publishers, a member of
Quarto Publishing Group USA Inc.
100 Cummings Center
Suite 406-L
Beverly, Massachusetts 01915-6101
Telephone: (978) 282-9590
Fax: (978) 283-2742
www.rockpub.com
Visit RockPaperInk.com to share your opinions, creations, and passion for design.

10 9 8 7 6 5 4 3 2

ISBN: 978-1-59253-803-4

Digital edition published in 2013
eISBN: 978-1-61058-786-0

Library of Congress Cataloging-in-Publication Data available

Design: Kathie Alexander

Printed in China

DEDICATION

Anika
(My eighteen-month-old daughter, who taught me that
simple things in life are the most beautiful.)

Lakshmi
(My wife, the most amazing person I have met in my life,
for being with me along this journey.)

CONTENTS

Adventures in Digital Design

The story of digital design begins at the user interface (UI); the point of contact between the user and a digital product. This book will take you on a journey, designing UIs for 100 digital products on a range of platforms, including the desktop, televisions, web, mobile devices, and tablets.

It will be a progressive journey where you will see how digital design has evolved from command-line interfaces, to graphical-user interfaces (GUIs), to natural interfaces, to multitouch and organic user interfaces. Along the way, you will learn how technological advances, such as capacitive touchscreens, Bluetooth, artificial intelligence, and text to speech, has molded the UI in innovative ways and taken digital design to a completely new level. It's a level where a designer must understand that the users and the context of the product dictate the design, and the success of a product is ultimately decided by user adoption.

Steve Jobs used to say, "Design is not what it looks like, design is how it works." This book will rip open the look of digital applications and take you behind the scenes. You'll discover how design works for 100 different digital applications, ranging from desktop software and widgets, to adaptive web interfaces, innovative mobiles apps, and games on tablets and televisions.

Using a practical approach to design principles, this book shows you how these principles can be applied to the latest digital products. You'll be guided through critical considerations for designing interfaces by showing you the big-picture: outlining the design guidelines and best practices while showing real examples of how these design principles can be successfully applied. Designers will get practical advice on developing a rich UI for everyday ad-hoc applications and the help they need in their daily job, thanks to these practical and invaluable examples, illustrations, and case studies.

1 User Interface (Human-Computer Interface)

THE MEANS BY WHICH A USER COMMUNICATES AND INTERACTS WITH A COMPUTER

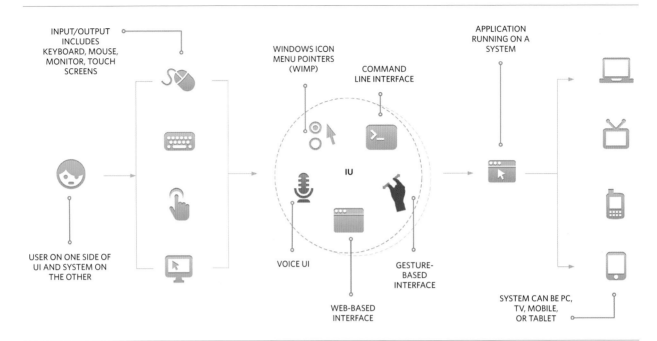

INPUT/OUTPUT INCLUDES KEYBOARD, MOUSE, MONITOR, TOUCH SCREENS

USER ON ONE SIDE OF UI AND SYSTEM ON THE OTHER

WINDOWS ICON MENU POINTERS (WIMP)

COMMAND LINE INTERFACE

IU

VOICE UI

GESTURE-BASED INTERFACE

WEB-BASED INTERFACE

APPLICATION RUNNING ON A SYSTEM

SYSTEM CAN BE PC, TV, MOBILE, OR TABLET

The user interface provides both the input mechanism, where the user "tells" the computer what the user needs, and an output mechanism, how the computer responds back to the user. People interact with a computer through a user interface using keyboard, mouse, touch screens, and microphone.

Best Practices and Design Guidelines
- Minimum Design
  - Use 80/20 rule, design for the top 20 percent features
  - Choose aesthetic colors and layout
  - Provide high noise-to-signal ratio between the chrome of the UI and data
- Simplicity
  - Keep design simple and clear
  - Focus on the main task and avoid user distraction
  - Keep functionality and simplicity

- Accessibility
  - Make easier to use and access by multiple devices, like old computers and assistive devices
  - Make usable by everyone: disabled, senior citizens, and people with low literacy level
- Consistency
  - Use similar layouts and terminology within the application
  - Employ familiar interaction and navigation
  - Keep the UI consistent within the context
- Feedback
  - Provide immediate feedback
  - Update user with current status for background actions
- Forgiveness
  - Allow for error prevention and allow undo
  - Limit user error by enabling on required commands
- User Driven
  - Give user complete control
  - Allow for customizability and personalization

(+) See also **Graphical User Interface (GUI)** on page 16, **Command Line Interface** on page 12, **WIMP Interface** on page 14, **Voice User Interface** on page 180, **Gesture-Based User Interface** on page 171, and **Web User Interface (WUI)** on page 48.

Microsoft Notepad

Notepad is one of the most used applications in Windows OS, whose UI has not changed in the past decade. The success of the application can be attributed to the simple and minimalistic UI design.

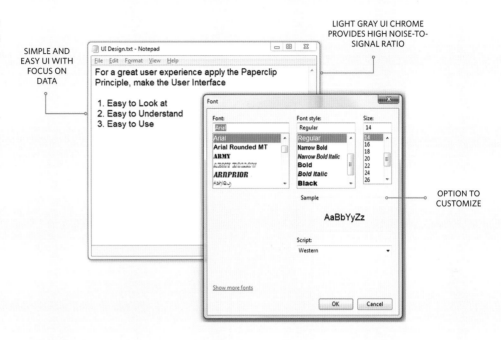

SIMPLE AND EASY UI WITH FOCUS ON DATA

LIGHT GRAY UI CHROME PROVIDES HIGH NOISE-TO-SIGNAL RATIO

OPTION TO CUSTOMIZE

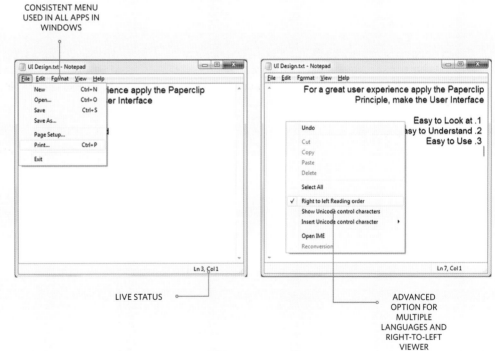

CONSISTENT MENU USED IN ALL APPS IN WINDOWS

LIVE STATUS

ADVANCED OPTION FOR MULTIPLE LANGUAGES AND RIGHT-TO-LEFT VIEWER

Command Line Interface (CLI)

A NONGRAPHICAL USER INTERFACE WHERE THE USER ENTERS COMMANDS TO INTERACT WITH APPLICATION

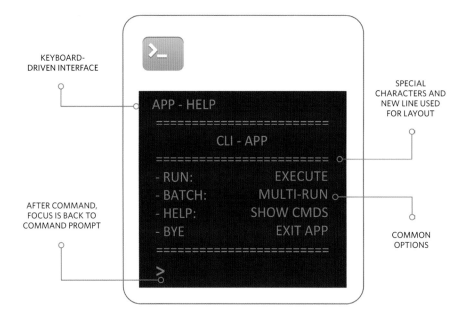

KEYBOARD-DRIVEN INTERFACE

SPECIAL CHARACTERS AND NEW LINE USED FOR LAYOUT

AFTER COMMAND, FOCUS IS BACK TO COMMAND PROMPT

COMMON OPTIONS

The CLI is a keyboard-driven text-based interface where the user types a line of commands with parameters, then presses enter to execute. The interface can be either interactive, where the user is prompted for more commands in a sequence, or noninteractive, where the program executes without further user intervention. The command line interface is popular for batch processes, when a single operation has to be applied multiple times.

Key Features and Functional Requirements
- Welcome screen with About information
- Screen for help command with details on each command and its parameters
- Menu with keyboard shortcuts

Best Practices and Design Guidelines
- Use standard verb-noun set "command parameter" (e.g., ftp> open http://google.com)
- Use keyboard shortcuts using letters or numbers to go to submenu
- Use full words for commands; avoid symbols and abbreviations (use delete instead of del)

- Use simple, easy-to-remember words for commands, such as "username" instead of "unique identifier"
- Give textual confirmation, feedback (when action is completed), and error messages
- Use font colors sparingly and avoid using for decoration

User Experience
- Update status and use percentage progress bars for background process
- On error, show comprehensive help commands with parameters
- Allow multiple parameters for batch operations
- Allow up and down arrow keys to access command history

(+) See also **Graphical User Interface (GUI)** on page 16.

Alpine (Email Client), University of Washington

Alpine uses a command line interface for email. It has a greeting message as a welcome screen and shows the command bar on the bottom, which changes based on the screen. The menu has options that can be reached using letter shortcuts. The interface is interactive and prompts the user at each screen to proceed.

COMMAND LINE INTERFACE FOR AN EMAIL CLIENT

WELCOME SCREEN WITH GREETING TEXT

QUICK COMMANDS FOR NEXT STEP

SIMPLE WHITE BACKGROUND WITH COLOR TO SEPARATE SPECIAL TEXT

MAIN MENU WITH ONE-LETTER SHORTCUT COMMANDS

ACTIVE PROMPT TO ENTER COMMAND

COMPREHENSIVE HELP

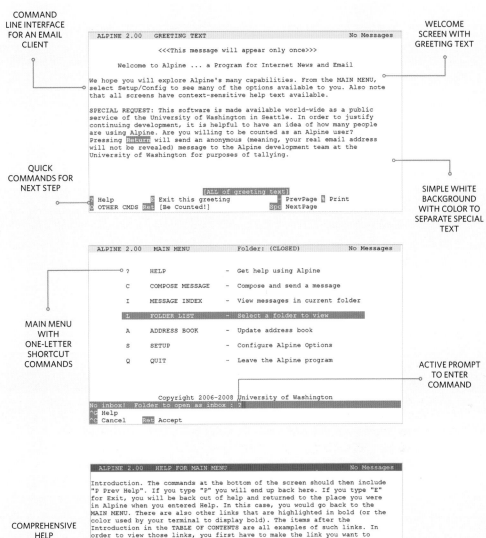

```
ALPINE 2.00    GREETING TEXT                              No Messages

             <<<This message will appear only once>>>

        Welcome to Alpine ... a Program for Internet News and Email

We hope you will explore Alpine's many capabilities. From the MAIN MENU,
select Setup/Config to see many of the options available to you. Also note
that all screens have context-sensitive help text available.

SPECIAL REQUEST: This software is made available world-wide as a public
service of the University of Washington in Seattle. In order to justify
continuing development, it is helpful to have an idea of how many people
are using Alpine. Are you willing to be counted as an Alpine user?
Pressing Return will send an anonymous (meaning, your real email address
will not be revealed) message to the Alpine development team at the
University of Washington for purposes of tallying.


                        [ALL of greeting text]
? Help          E Exit this greeting              - PrevPage N Print
C OTHER CMDS Ret [Be Counted!]                  Spc NextPage
```

```
ALPINE 2.00    MAIN MENU            Folder: (CLOSED)        No Messages

    ?    HELP              - Get help using Alpine

    C    COMPOSE MESSAGE   - Compose and send a message

    I    MESSAGE INDEX     - View messages in current folder

    L    FOLDER LIST       - Select a folder to view

    A    ADDRESS BOOK      - Update address book

    S    SETUP             - Configure Alpine Options

    Q    QUIT              - Leave the Alpine program


              Copyright 2006-2008 University of Washington
No inbox!  Folder to open as inbox : ?
^G Help
^C Cancel     Ret Accept
```

```
ALPINE 2.00   HELP FOR MAIN MENU                          No Messages

Introduction. The commands at the bottom of the screen should then include
"P Prev Help". If you type "P" you will end up back here. If you type "E"
for Exit, you will be back out of help and returned to the place you were
in Alpine when you entered Help. In this case, you would go back to the
MAIN MENU. There are also other links that are highlighted in bold (or the
color used by your terminal to display bold). The items after the
Introduction in the TABLE OF CONTENTS are all examples of such links. In
order to view those links, you first have to make the link you want to
view the current link. The "NextLink" and "PrevLink" commands (see bottom
of screen) can do that for you.

TABLE OF CONTENTS

1. Introduction
2. Alpine Help
3. Giving Commands in Alpine
4. Alpine Configuration
5. Titlebar Line
6. Main Menu

M Main Menu E Exit Help     P PrevLink      - PrevPage N Print
? Help Help  V [View Link] ^B NextLink    Spc NextPage Z Print All  W WhereIs
```

WINDOWS, ICONS, MENUS, AND POINTER-BASED INTERFACE

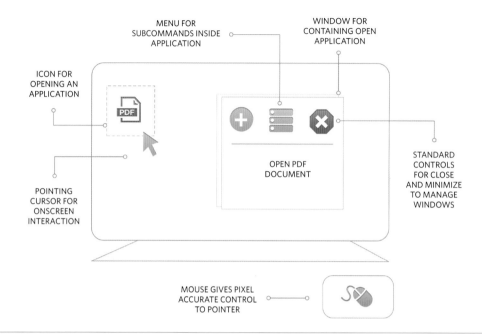

MENU FOR SUBCOMMANDS INSIDE APPLICATION

WINDOW FOR CONTAINING OPEN APPLICATION

ICON FOR OPENING AN APPLICATION

OPEN PDF DOCUMENT

STANDARD CONTROLS FOR CLOSE AND MINIMIZE TO MANAGE WINDOWS

POINTING CURSOR FOR ONSCREEN INTERACTION

MOUSE GIVES PIXEL ACCURATE CONTROL TO POINTER

A WIMP interface was the early evolution of the GUI, which was based on the use of a mouse, along with key UI elements, windows, clickable icons, and pull-down menus. Windows run self-contained programs, icons were meant to be clicked for execution, menus provide a readily available list of commands, and pointers (cursors) allow the user to visually track the mouse.

Best Practices and Design Guidelines
- Allow manipulation of windows with options to close, minimize, and resize
- Allow "what you see is what you get" (WYSWYG) interaction with pixel-accurate interaction
- Use naming conventions as nouns for objects and verbs for actions in menus and commands
- Give user control and keep a dialogue of request and response between user and computer
- Create a forgiving user interface that allows users to undo

User expectation from a WIMP interface is consistency between the user interface and interactions.

User Experience
- Use consistent design with familiar icons and menu options
- Give feedback and keep users informed about progress
- Allow the movement of content within the window, which can be scrolled
- Use title bars to recognize the window

(+) See also **Graphical User Interface (GUI)** on page 16 and **Command Line Interface** on page 12.

Home Screen for Xerox Star (1981) and Apple Lisa Computer (1984)

WIMP interface was used in Star computers to manage multiple programs. It had small graphical images (icons) that represented individual programs as well as files and directory commands.

The Apple Lisa computer featured a set of icons, windows with menus, and a pointer to interact with them. The design was easy to learn and was consistently applied across all applications in the computer.

WINDOW WITH AN OPEN SAMPLE DOCUMENT IN XEROX STAR

ICONS TO INTERACT WITH THE COMPUTER FILE SYSTEM AND OPEN PROGRAMS

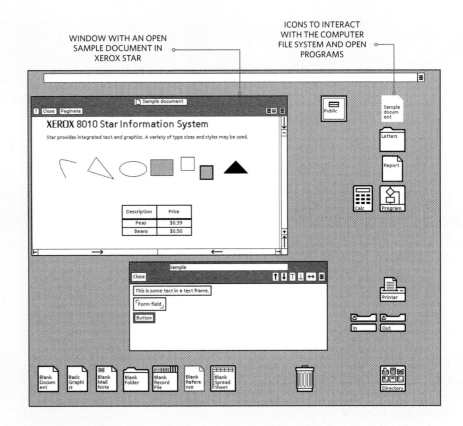

POINTING CURSOR CONTROLLED BY THE MOUSE

MENUS AND SUBMENUS FOR COMMANDS

APPLICATION ICONS IN APPLE LISA COMPUTER

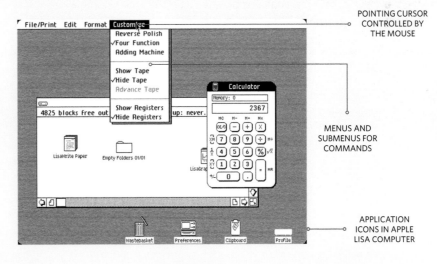

Graphical User Interface (GUI)

AN INTERFACE TO INTERACT WITH COMPUTERS USING PICTURES AND SYMBOLS

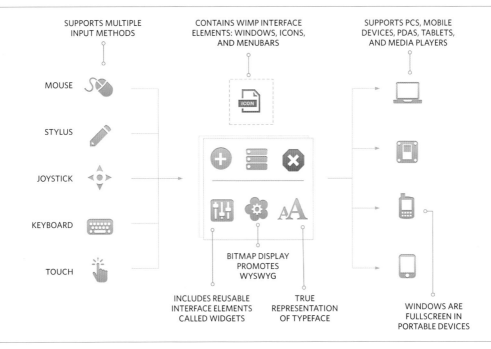

SUPPORTS MULTIPLE INPUT METHODS

MOUSE
STYLUS
JOYSTICK
KEYBOARD
TOUCH

CONTAINS WIMP INTERFACE ELEMENTS: WINDOWS, ICONS, AND MENUBARS

SUPPORTS PCS, MOBILE DEVICES, PDAS, TABLETS, AND MEDIA PLAYERS

INCLUDES REUSABLE INTERFACE ELEMENTS CALLED WIDGETS

BITMAP DISPLAY PROMOTES WYSWYG

TRUE REPRESENTATION OF TYPEFACE

WINDOWS ARE FULLSCREEN IN PORTABLE DEVICES

A graphical user interface, or GUI (pronounced "gooey"), is the evolution of the WIMP (windows, icons, menus, and pointers) interface to include reusable UI elements and supports mobile devices (phones, PDAs, and music players) that don't necessarily use mouse pointers. It allows you to interact with the application using graphical images, icons, and elements on the 2-D screen, without having to memorize complicated commands and type them precisely using a keyboard, as in command line interface (CLI).

Best Practices and Design Guidelines

- Use metaphors and choose similar real-world names to associate with the application, such as folders, desktop, and office applications
- Make sure the user can anticipate a UI element behavior from its visual properties
- Convey warnings, errors, etc. in understandable language with visual cues and icons
- Use consistent theme for the windows and UI elements and their behaviors
- Use familiar images and actions to make it understandable, such as home icon to go to main window
- Create reusable UI elements, including basic controls like buttons, input box, and message boxes
- Make sure the interface gives feedback on user's actions and keep the user updated with the status in a friendly, predictable, and familiar way

(+) See also **WIMP Interface** on page 14, **Command Line Interface** on page 12, and **Integrated Development Environment** (IDE) on page 26.

Microsoft Visual Studio 2012

Microsoft Visual Studio 2012 integrated development environment (IDE) is GUI based and allows developers to create applications. It uses a familiar window, menu, and icon–based approach for interface design and allows users to manage project files using tabs and explorers, which is predictable and familiar to a Windows user.

VISUAL STUDIO 2012 IS A GUI-BASED IDE

MAIN WINDOW TO CONTAIN ALL FILES OF THE PROJECT

TABS TO KEEP THE CURRENT INFORMATION ON THE TOP

STANDARD TOOLBARS AND MENU-BASED COMMANDS

ALLOWS THE REUSABLE INTERFACE ELEMENTS TO USE IN APPLICATION DEVELOPMENT

WHAT YOU SEE IS WHAT YOU GET EDITOR

TREE VIEW PROJECT STRUCTURE SIMILAR TO WINDOWS EXPLORER

CONSISTENT COLOR THEME FOR ALL UI ELEMENTS

SCROLLBARS FOR MORE INFORMATION

AESTHETIC LOOK, DESPITE A LOT OF ELEMENTS ON THE SCREEN

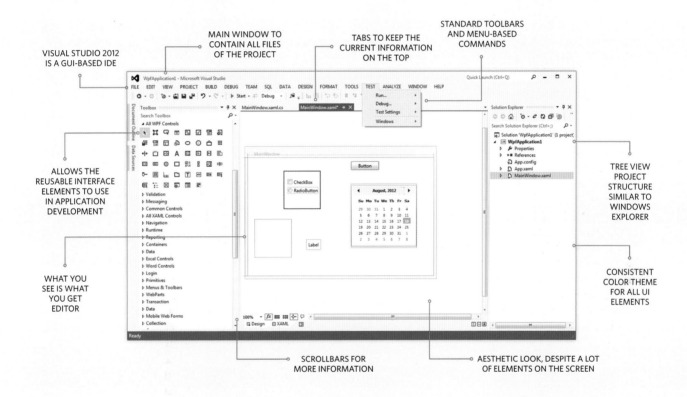

5 Photo Editor

A GRAPHICS APPLICATION USED FOR ENHANCING AND EDITING DIGITAL IMAGES

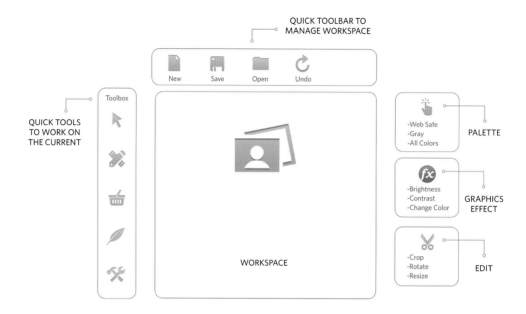

A photo editor is meant for editing or adding effects to an existing image (raster graphics). A photo editor is a sophisticated GUI-based application and has numerous graphic filters that can be applied to an existing image to enhance it.

Key Features and Functional Requirements
- Big workspace for working on single image
- Standard application toolbar for quickly accessing, creating, and saving files
- Toolbox for quick editing and color palette for selecting and changing colors
- Option to add layers and graphic effects
- Editing features like crop, resize, and rotate
- Advanced editors contains histogram of image as well as other imaging capabilities

Best Practices and Design Guidelines
- Use a full-screen interface (the standard practice) with optimum space for the workspace
- Use floating, hideable components for color palettes, toolbox, and graphic effects
- Provide option to work on multiple images simultaneously with tabs interface
- Give quick access to image dimension and zoom view to help designers work efficiently
- Provide advanced options like preview when applying graphic filters
- Offer quick access to most-used editing features like crop, resize, and rotate

(+) See also **Image Manager** on page 20.

Paint.NET Image Editor

Paint.NET is a GUI-based image editor with advanced graphic features. The UI uses a standard toolbar for managing workspace and has dynamic floating UI components for tool-box, layers, color palette, etc. It has a center workspace and shows image dimension, zoom view, and preview while working. The UI is clean and allows designers to work on the image unobtrusively.

TOOLBAR FOR MANAGING WORKSPACE

QUICK PREVIEW AND HISTORY

TOOLBOX FOR QUICK EDITING

COLOR PALETTE

LAYERS AND EFFECTS

BIG WORKSPACE FOR IMAGE EDITING

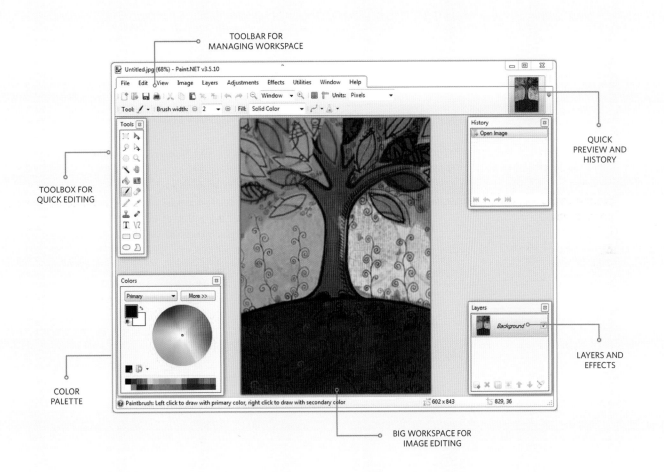

Image Manager

AN APPLICATION THAT HELPS ORGANIZE IMAGES

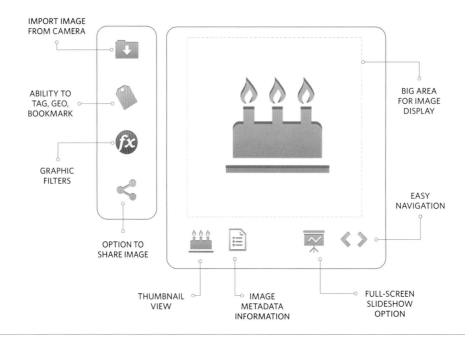

IMPORT IMAGE
FROM CAMERA

ABILITY TO
TAG, GEO,
BOOKMARK

GRAPHIC
FILTERS

OPTION TO
SHARE IMAGE

BIG AREA
FOR IMAGE
DISPLAY

EASY
NAVIGATION

THUMBNAIL
VIEW

IMAGE
METADATA
INFORMATION

FULL-SCREEN
SLIDESHOW
OPTION

An image manager helps you manage your images in a single place. It allows you to browse through your computer for images, has basic image-editing functionalities like red-eye removal, and helps create a slideshow of images.

Best Practices and Design Guidelines

- Have a gallery, list, icon, and detailed view for selected folder in the browser
- Allow thumbnails and quick metadata for selected images
- Use a single-image view screen for image editing and quick navigation
- Allow for best fit (default), original size, full screen, and fit screen for image display
- Allow for basic image-editing capability like contrast, brightness, cropping, and red-eye removal

User expectations from an image manager are quick browsing and the ability to go through metadata, add tags, and share.

⊕ See also **Explorer** on page 22, **Slideshow** on page 104, and **Mobile Photo App** on page 128.

Image Manager

Image manager is a simple image organizer with an integrated explorer view to go through folders in a computer. It instantly displays all the image files in the folder in a gallery view. It also has a list view, an icon view, and a detailed view for faster loading. There's also a thumbnail view for the selected images with metadata. The Image manager also allows users to share the images on the web.

SHARE IMAGES ON THE WEB

INTEGRATED EXPLORER TO BROWSE YOUR COMPUTER FOR IMAGES

THUMBNAIL OF SELECTED IMAGE IN THE BROWSER

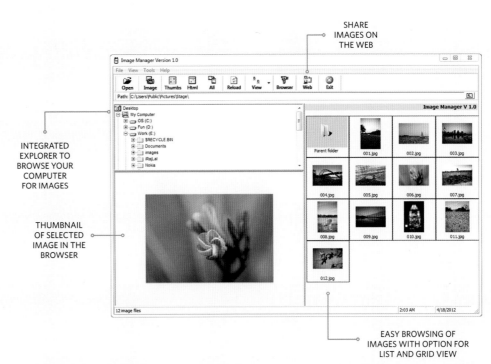

EASY BROWSING OF IMAGES WITH OPTION FOR LIST AND GRID VIEW

EASY NAVIGATION TO IMAGES IN THE FOLDER

FULL-SCREEN DISPLAY WITH MULTIPLE SIZE OPTIONS

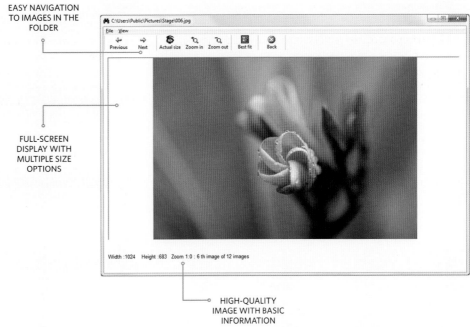

HIGH-QUALITY IMAGE WITH BASIC INFORMATION

Desktop Explorer

AN APPLICATION THAT HELPS ORGANIZE YOUR FILES AND FOLDERS

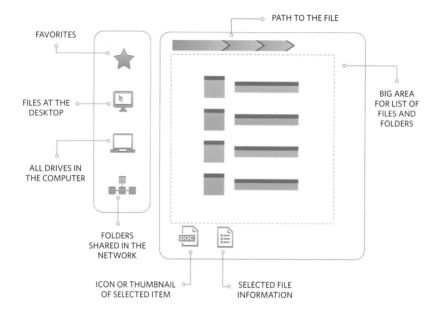

An explorer helps you navigate files and folders in your computer. It is a file browser and management utility that uses a hierarchal navigation system. It has thumbnail previews of pictures and files and has a filter-based file browser. An explorer helps you check a file's metadata such as name, file size, date created, and media information, and preview thumbnails.

Key Features and Functional Requirements

- Customizable list, grid, thumbnail, and detail view for list of files
- Tree structure for directory hierarchy and navigation
- Breadcrumbs UI controls for current path of the selected items
- Information bar for selected files' metadata
- Optional thumbnail or icon preview

Best Practices and Design Guidelines

- Use familiar computer icon for folder hierarchy
- Allow filtering of list of files and multiple thumbnail view of files
- Use breadcrumb navigation, which has become a standard for file path
- Make control similar to the explorer in the computer
- Allow preview of files and quick file information

User expectations from an explorer are fast performance and familiar experience.

(+) See also **Image Manager** on page 20 and **Touch User Interface** on page 166.

Windows Explorer Control and Touch Screen Explorer

Windows explorer control uses a standard treelike structure for displaying the hierarchy of folders in the computer and allows the user to access frequently used folders like my documents and desktops. It also allows for the creation of a custom shortcut to frequently used folders. On the other hand, the touch screen explorer is optimized for touch and tap and uses bigger icons for files and folders. It uses a simple list view with thumbnails instead of a directory tree.

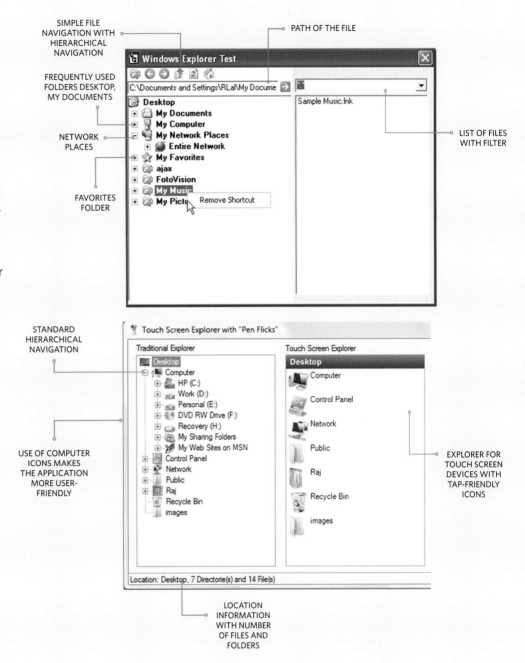

SIMPLE FILE NAVIGATION WITH HIERARCHICAL NAVIGATION

PATH OF THE FILE

FREQUENTLY USED FOLDERS DESKTOP, MY DOCUMENTS

NETWORK PLACES

FAVORITES FOLDER

LIST OF FILES WITH FILTER

STANDARD HIERARCHICAL NAVIGATION

USE OF COMPUTER ICONS MAKES THE APPLICATION MORE USER-FRIENDLY

EXPLORER FOR TOUCH SCREEN DEVICES WITH TAP-FRIENDLY ICONS

LOCATION INFORMATION WITH NUMBER OF FILES AND FOLDERS

8 Assistant/Software Wizard

A SOFTWARE TOOL TO GUIDE YOU THROUGH A MULTIPLE-STEP PROCESS

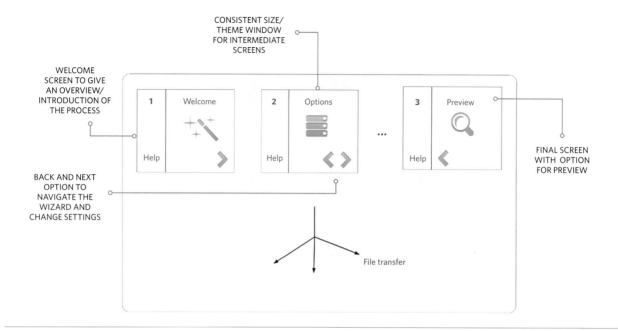

An assistant (also called a software wizard) is meant to help a user with a complex task, such as setting up an application or creating a video, or a task that normally requires the user to choose multiple settings, by asking a set of questions and presenting default options. It helps first-time users get acquainted with the process. The wizard also allows users to go back into the steps and change things.

Best Practices and Design Guidelines

- Keep a welcome/introduction screen to give an overview of the process
- Make sure all the steps in the assistant are divided into logical categories
- Give a consistent look, feel, and size for each dialog box with a standard icon for a feeling of a flow
- Provide onscreen help for each step or link to help documentation
- Make selections function between forward and backward navigation
- Have recommended settings with default-selected choices for fast process

(+) See also **Graphical User Interface (GUI)** on page 16 and **WIMP Interface** on page 14.

Migration Assistant in Mac

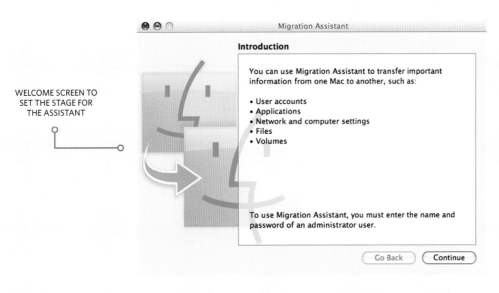

WELCOME SCREEN TO
SET THE STAGE FOR
THE ASSISTANT

The migration assistant on the Macintosh operating system allows users to transfer their documents and settings to a new Mac computer. It presents the user with easy choices and allows for both forward and backward navigation.

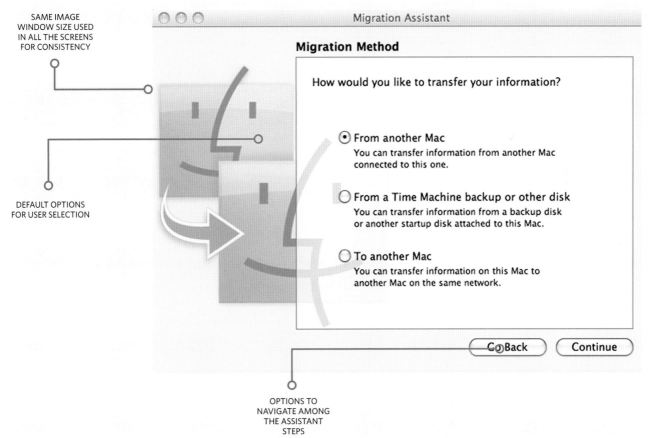

SAME IMAGE
WINDOW SIZE USED
IN ALL THE SCREENS
FOR CONSISTENCY

DEFAULT OPTIONS
FOR USER SELECTION

OPTIONS TO
NAVIGATE AMONG
THE ASSISTANT
STEPS

Integrated Development Environment (IDE)

AN APPLICATION WITH INTEGRATED TOOLS AND LIBRARIES TO HELP PROGRAMMERS OPTIMIZE THEIR WORKFLOW

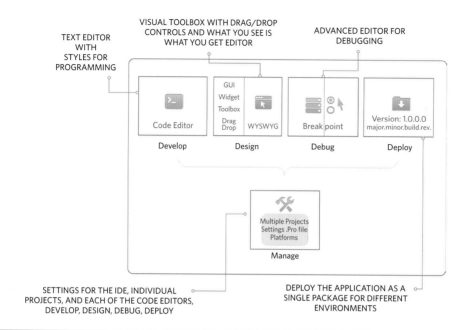

An integrated development environment (IDE) is a GUI-based framework that improves productivity by automating repetitive tasks and giving easy access to reusable controls, libraries, and functionalities. It helps in the complete software development life cycle by integrating all the tools required by a programmer in a single application to help design, develop, debug, and deploy an application.

Best Practices and Design Guidelines
- Have a source code/text editor with color coding
- Have an option to show and hide individual IDE windows like toolbox, output window, and designer
- Allow line numbers and collapsible code view
- Provide a project explorer and settings to easily access multiple projects
- Provide ability to debug, deploy, search, etc, without leaving the coding environment
- Provide ease of access to the most frequently used features

(+) See also **Assistant/Software Wizard** on page 24 and **Graphical User Interface (GUI)** on page 16.

Qt Creator IDE

TREE VIEW TO
MANAGE MULTIPLE
PROJECTS

COLOR CODING
PROVIDES A VISUAL
CLUE FOR DEVELOPERS
FOR KEYWORDS AND
FUNCTIONS

Qt Creator IDE creates GUI applications that run on multiple operating systems and devices. It allows you to manage multiple projects in the explorer view and have a comprehensive source code editor with line numbers and the option to collapse the code section. It also integrates compiler output, application output, search, and project settings in the IDE.

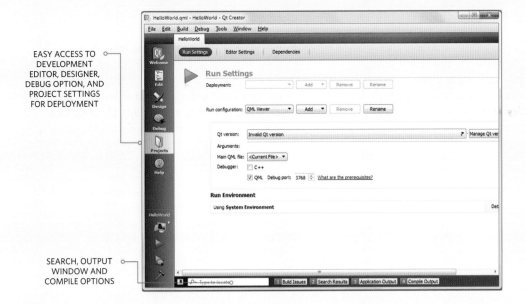

EASY ACCESS TO
DEVELOPMENT
EDITOR, DESIGNER,
DEBUG OPTION, AND
PROJECT SETTINGS
FOR DEPLOYMENT

SEARCH, OUTPUT
WINDOW AND
COMPILE OPTIONS

Media Player

AN APPLICATION THAT PLAYS AUDIO AND VIDEO FILES

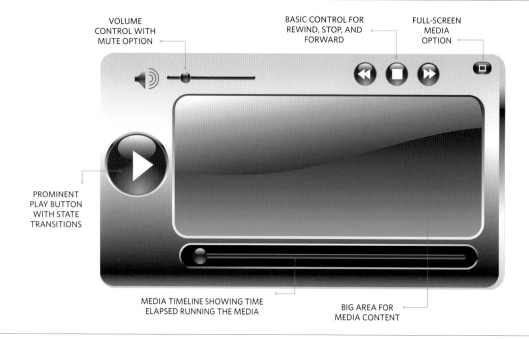

VOLUME CONTROL WITH MUTE OPTION

BASIC CONTROL FOR REWIND, STOP, AND FORWARD

FULL-SCREEN MEDIA OPTION

PROMINENT PLAY BUTTON WITH STATE TRANSITIONS

MEDIA TIMELINE SHOWING TIME ELAPSED RUNNING THE MEDIA

BIG AREA FOR MEDIA CONTENT

A media player is a simple utility that plays a media file. It can be part of a bigger media application like iTunes, Windows Media Player, or Winamp, which provides other media management and editing capabilities. A media player is also used as a plug-in application inside a web browser. It normally comes with standard TV controls to play, pause, forward, and rewind the media file.

Best Practices and Design Guidelines

- Create a media player with a rich interface with advanced state and transitions
- Use high-quality images for controls with transparency and gradients
- Provide a timeline with duration information to show the time elapsed while viewing the media
- Have visible volume controls with a quick mute option
- Allow customization with "skins" or themes to change the look and feel of the player
- Have a basic version with the most common options for quick playing
- Have a prominent play button and a button to go full screen

⊕ See also **Rich Internet Application (RIA)** on page 96 and **Web Widget** on page 98.

Vimeo.com is a video-sharing website and features an advanced online media player that allows for video upload, sharing, and viewing. It provides a rich media player for all the uploaded videos and allows for custom size as well as high-definition playback. It uses a default image for the video unless a thumbnail is generated by the video's originator.

MEDIA PLAYER AT VIMEO.COM

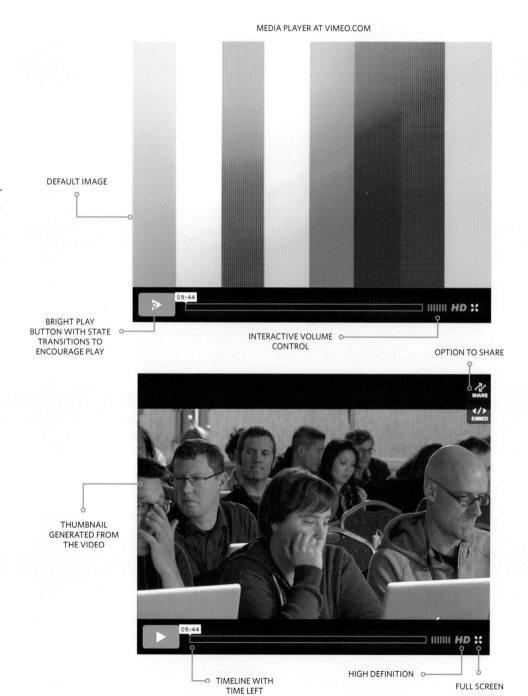

DEFAULT IMAGE

BRIGHT PLAY BUTTON WITH STATE TRANSITIONS TO ENCOURAGE PLAY

INTERACTIVE VOLUME CONTROL

OPTION TO SHARE

THUMBNAIL GENERATED FROM THE VIDEO

TIMELINE WITH TIME LEFT

HIGH DEFINITION

FULL SCREEN

11 Desktop Widget/Gadget

A LIGHTWEIGHT APPLICATION ON USER'S DESKTOP FOR READY-TO-USE INFORMATION AND FEATURES

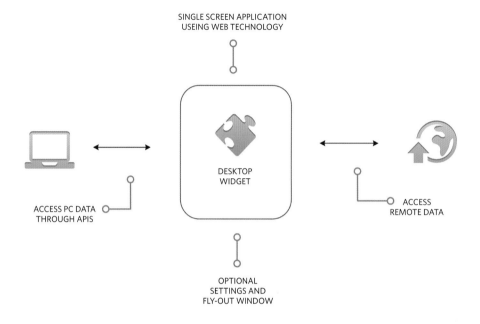

SINGLE SCREEN APPLICATION
USEING WEB TECHNOLOGY

DESKTOP
WIDGET

ACCESS PC DATA
THROUGH APIS

ACCESS
REMOTE DATA

OPTIONAL
SETTINGS AND
FLY-OUT WINDOW

A desktop widget/gadget is a mini application meant for quick information, small utilities, games, and accessories to an existing application or web service. It gives at-a-glance information and allows easy access to useful features. Widgets can be clocks, calculators, games, sticky notes, and more. Desktop widgets use web technology to render information, and they are easy to develop. They don't use standard UI elements like dialog boxes with menus, toolbars, and windows.

The purpose of a widget is brief information for further action.

Best Practices and Design Guidelines
- Target a specific task with a simple user interface
- Allow quick access to dynamic live data
- Show only relevant information, avoid scroll bars
- Use consistent visuals for reload, error, information, and warnings
- Avoid advertisement in the widget
- Use visuals, images, signs, icons, and color to give visual clues of the functionality
- Keep interaction elements in a widget unobtrusive
- Have default settings for first-time users

(+) See also **Graphical User Interface (GUI)** on page 16 and **Web Widget** on page 98.

A Trick of the Day Gadget

Trick of Mind (found at TrickofMind.com) is an information gadget that pulls RSS feed and shows the title of the everyday trick puzzles in a quick and easy way on the gadget screen. It features a fly-out window for details of the puzzle and a setting screen for customizing the layout.

SIMPLE MAIN SCREEN OF THE GADGET WITH QUICK TITLES

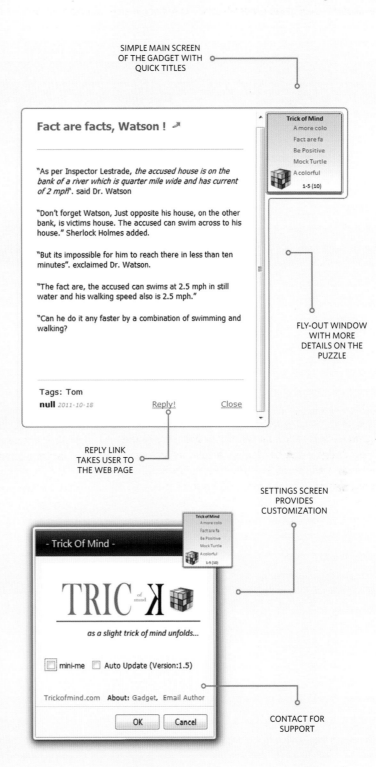

Fact are facts, Watson ! ↗

"As per Inspector Lestrade, *the accused house is on the bank of a river which is quarter mile wide and has current of 2 mph*". said Dr. Watson

"Don't forget Watson, Just opposite his house, on the other bank, is victims house. The accused can swim across to his house." Sherlock Holmes added.

"But its impossible for him to reach there in less than ten minutes". exclaimed Dr. Watson.

"The fact are, the accused can swims at 2.5 mph in still water and his walking speed also is 2.5 mph."

"Can he do it any faster by a combination of swimming and walking?

Tags: Tom
null *2011-10-18*   Reply!   Close

FLY-OUT WINDOW WITH MORE DETAILS ON THE PUZZLE

REPLY LINK TAKES USER TO THE WEB PAGE

SETTINGS SCREEN PROVIDES CUSTOMIZATION

- Trick Of Mind -

TRIC of mind K

as a slight trick of mind unfolds...

☐ mini-me   ☐ Auto Update (Version:1.5)

Trickofmind.com   **About:** Gadget, Email Author

OK   Cancel

CONTACT FOR SUPPORT

Dashboard/Scorecards

A DASHBOARD PROVIDES A QUICK VIEW OF ALL KEY INFORMATION IN A SYSTEM

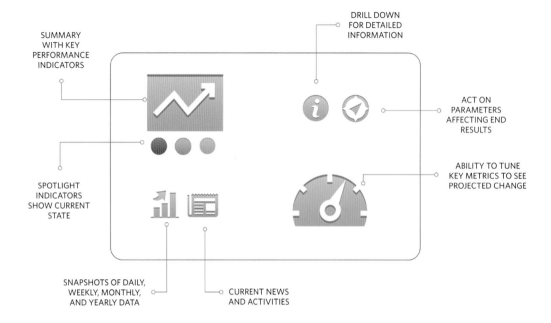

SUMMARY WITH KEY PERFORMANCE INDICATORS

DRILL DOWN FOR DETAILED INFORMATION

ACT ON PARAMETERS AFFECTING END RESULTS

ABILITY TO TUNE KEY METRICS TO SEE PROJECTED CHANGE

SPOTLIGHT INDICATORS SHOW CURRENT STATE

SNAPSHOTS OF DAILY, WEEKLY, MONTHLY, AND YEARLY DATA

CURRENT NEWS AND ACTIVITIES

A dashboard/scorecard interface shows key performance indicators of a system in a visually understandable way. It surfaces summaries, trends, statistical data, and issue areas to help the user make informed decisions. Similar to an automobile dashboard, a digital dashboard helps monitor and interpret information by showing a quick view of the whole system.

Best Practices and Design Guidelines
- Have a single page with multiple blocks of visual information
- Keep the most important data or summary on the top left panel
- Keep the interface simple and data organized around key metrics
- Use ranking and highlighting for showing current performance
- Add interactive controls to change key metrics to project final output
- Keep interactive tools clearly marked and keep old data to compare for change

User expectations from a dashboard are quick information and the to ability to change data for projection and estimates.

User Experience
- Create an aesthetically pleasing overall design
- Have a summary block for quick overview of key performance indicators
- Provide short, precise, and easily readable text
- Use bar graph for statistics data and charts to visualize data
- Show more information such as relative data, which helps with business decisions

(+) See also **Homepage** on page 54 and **Single-Page Website** on page 58.

InfraDashboard by Infragistic Labs

The dashboard by Infragistic provides a one-page view of their financial information system. It uses panels for summary, key metrics, performance, and statistical data. The overall design is simple, with a plain theme. Bright colors direct attention to important data.

CURRENT NEWS

QUICK SUMMARY WITH KEY METRICS

DRILL DOWN

STATISTICAL DATA ON PERFORMANCE

GAUGE VIEW WITH HISTORICAL DATA

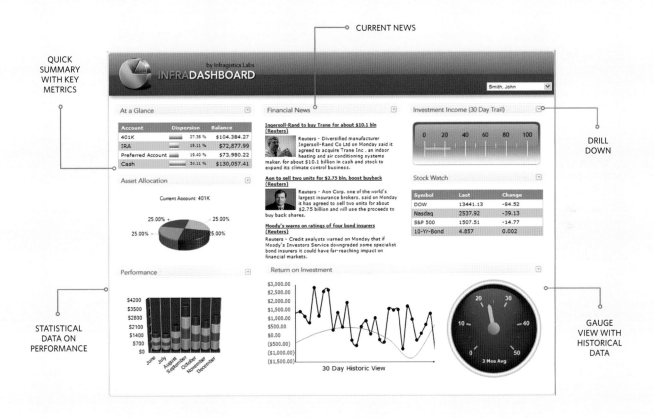

Instant Messenger (IM)

AN APPLICATION FOR REMOTE CHAT BETWEEN TWO PEOPLE

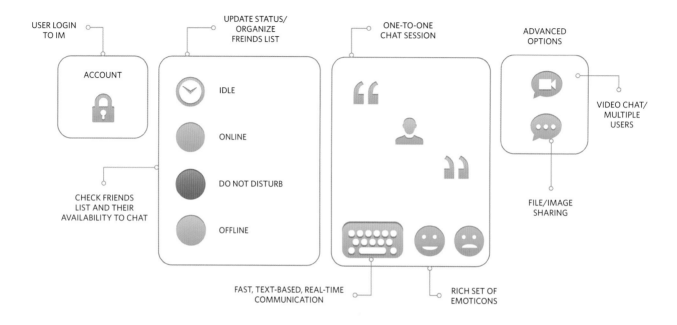

Instant messenger provides a fast, text-based, real-time communication channel over the Internet. It creates a private chat session between two users who are using the messenger client application. The traditional IM software is desktop based, but now it has become an integral part of websites and even smartphones.

Best Practices and Design Guidelines
- Keep IM as a single-purpose application with a compact interface
- Support for rich text formatting and emoticons in the message
- Allow option to set user status, profile picture, and availability
- Provide a rich set of text-based emoticons for chat
- Have little branding and advertisement

User expectation from an instant messenger is personal, quick, and reliable communication.

User Experience
- Clean with minimum distraction
- Engaging conversations with pictures, multimedia, and file-sharing support
- Personalized expression with profile image, formatted text, fonts, and themes
- Options for login and log chat

(+) See also **Chat Room** on page 35 and **Video Chat** on page 36.

Chat Room

A CHAT APPLICATION TO COMMUNICATE REMOTELY WITH A GROUP OF PEOPLE

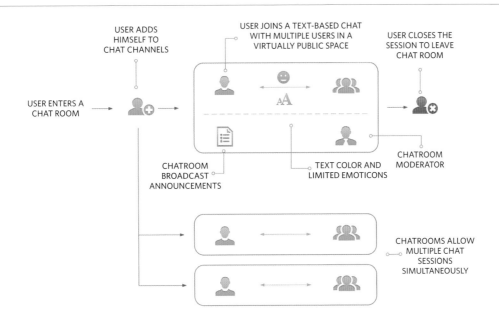

USER ADDS HIMSELF TO CHAT CHANNELS

USER JOINS A TEXT-BASED CHAT WITH MULTIPLE USERS IN A VIRTUALLY PUBLIC SPACE

USER CLOSES THE SESSION TO LEAVE CHAT ROOM

USER ENTERS A CHAT ROOM

CHATROOM MODERATOR

CHATROOM BROADCAST ANNOUNCEMENTS

TEXT COLOR AND LIMITED EMOTICONS

CHATROOMS ALLOW MULTIPLE CHAT SESSIONS SIMULTANEOUSLY

A chat room is an interactive forum where you can chat with multiple users in real time. A chat room does not necessarily need the user to log in to a service; the user can go to a particular chat room by opening an instance of that chat room (also called a channel) and becoming an active member. Unlike instant messengers, chat rooms allow limited personalization in terms of profile pictures, emoticons, and message formatting.

Best Practices and Design Guidelines

- List available chat rooms to join and allow user to create new chat rooms
- Avoid registration/login for public chat rooms
- Allow public and private text-based chatting with guest access
- Allow status indicators and user profiles with nick-names/avatars
- Provide option to accept/ignore messages from users not on the user's contact list
- Have welcome message with chat room rules for new users
- Provide an easy method to contact chat room moderator
- Make chat accessible only from keyboard
- Use minimal text-based advertising

+ See also **Instant Messenger (IM)** on page 34 and **Online Forums** on page 80.

15 Video Chat

COMMUNICATION SOFTWARE WITH WEB CAMERA

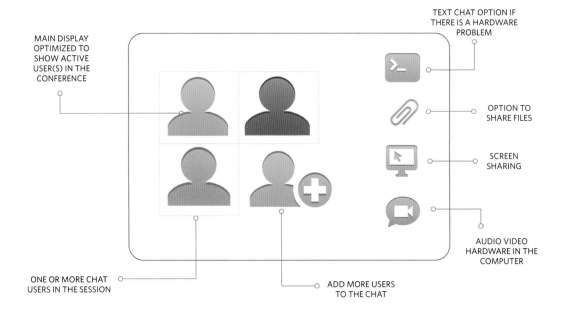

TEXT CHAT OPTION IF THERE IS A HARDWARE PROBLEM

MAIN DISPLAY OPTIMIZED TO SHOW ACTIVE USER(S) IN THE CONFERENCE

OPTION TO SHARE FILES

SCREEN SHARING

AUDIO VIDEO HARDWARE IN THE COMPUTER

ONE OR MORE CHAT USERS IN THE SESSION

ADD MORE USERS TO THE CHAT

A video chat is an interactive application that allows two or more people to communicate with live sound and video. It uses the computer's web camera and audio device for two-way audio and video transmission.

Best Practices and Design Guidelines
- Optimize display for showing one or more users
- Have easy option to add/invite more users to the conference
- Use standard chat options to share screen, files, etc.
- Provide controls for changing hardware settings
- Enable users to add users from existing contacts
- Provide quick option for volume and file sharing
- Allow users to position user view and change it to full screen
- Keep the call window at a fixed place and video at the foreground
- If using controls on top of video, use transparent controls with borders

User expectations from a video chat room are quick collaboration and seamless interaction. They want to spend less time configuring the software and more time chatting.

User Experience
- Easy-to-use video conferencing
- Minimum or automatic configuration for audio/video
- Little or no advertising
- Option for screen sharing
- Maximize display window for video

(+) See also **Instant Messenger (IM)** on page 34 and **Chat Room** on page 35.

ooVoo Video Chat

The video chat application by ooVoo is a simple-to-use application and allows up to twelve-way video chat. After users log in to their account, they can add users by email account. It also allows users with no camera support in the conference by offering a text chat option. The UI is simple and the display is optimized for video conferencing with multiple users. The chat client also has the option to share screens and files.

TEXT CHAT FOR USERS WITH NO AUDIO, VIDEO SUPPORT

SCREEN SHARE OPTION

MULTIPLE ACTIVE SESSIONS

MAIN DISPLAY WITH ACTIVE USERS

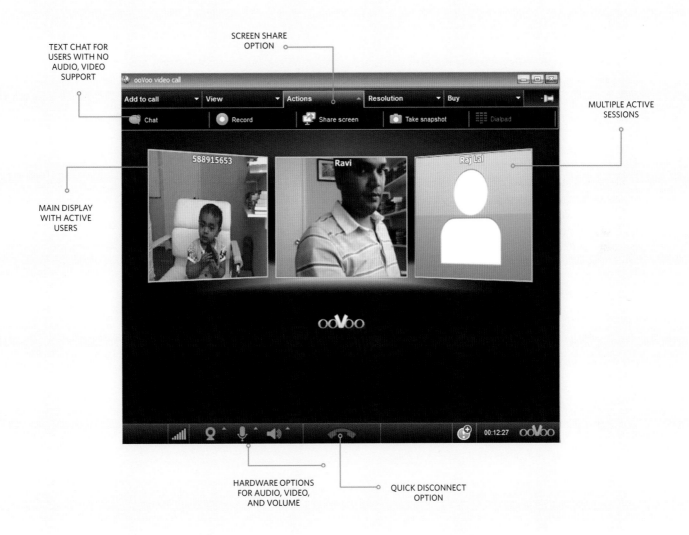

HARDWARE OPTIONS FOR AUDIO, VIDEO, AND VOLUME

QUICK DISCONNECT OPTION

Interactive Voice Response (IVR) System

AN AUTOMATED TELEPHONY SYSTEM THAT INTERACTS WITH CALLERS

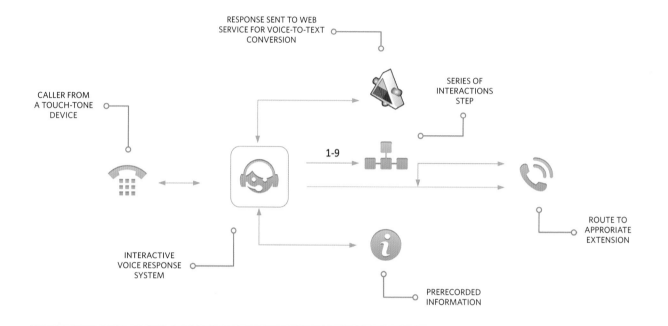

An interactive voice response (IVR) system uses prerecorded voice responses to collect information from the caller and routes them. The IVR system is used for call forwarding, looking up information, troubleshooting, and automated 24/7 customer service. The IVR system accepts voice or touch-tone input, processes them, and forwards the caller accordingly. It acts as a virtual information desk.

Best Practices and Design Guidelines
- Have fully defined decision tree to guide the caller with predefined steps
- Order steps according to the frequency of calls
- Have standard options such as:
    - Maximum of four options at every step
    - "0" for representative, "#" for repeat
- Use simple user interface to configure IVR system
- Allow integration with database and web services

User expectation from an IVR system is a complete set of tools for full customization.

User Experience
- Welcome user and try to add some personality to IVR system
- Use a female voice with clear accent for prerecorded messages
- Craft simple messages
- Include default options for no entry

Keep menu prompts short and concise

(+) See also **Voice User Interface** on page 180 and **Intelligent User Interface** on page 198.

Voicent IVR System

Voicent IVR is an easy-to-use interactive voice system that can be easily integrated with a telephony system as well as Java-based applications that can connect to databases. The application provides a visual flow for creating steps in the IVR system and comes with tutorials to help the user configure the system successfully.

COMPREHENSIVE TUTORIAL ON SETTING UP INTERACTIVE VOICE RESPONSE SYSTEM

QUICK HOW-TO TUTORIALS FOR EACH FUNCTIONALITY

START PAGE FOR FIRST-TIME USERS

STEP-BY-STEP INSTRUCTIONS FOR IVR SYSTEM

INTEGRATED WITH SOFTWARE APPLICATION TO QUERY DATABASE

EASY-TO-CREATE VISUAL SETUP FOR USER INTERACTION

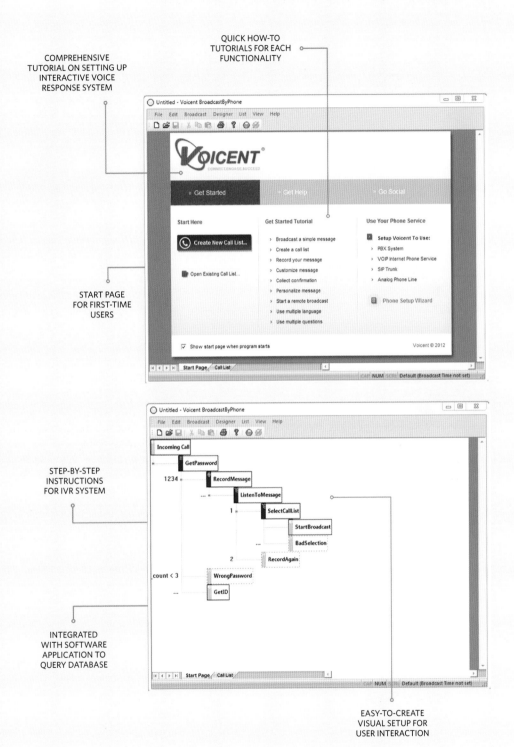

Direct User Interface

AN APPLICATION THAT ALLOWS USERS TO DIRECTLY INTERACT WITH THE INTERFACE

DIRECT INTERFACE
WITH 3-D OBJECT

USER CAN INTERACT WITH OBJECT BY
DIRECTLY MANIPULATING THE SURFACE

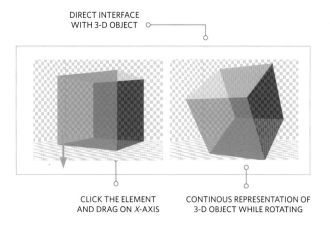

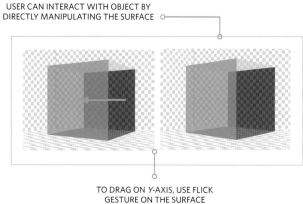

CLICK THE ELEMENT
AND DRAG ON *X*-AXIS

CONTINOUS REPRESENTATION OF
3-D OBJECT WHILE ROTATING

TO DRAG ON *Y*-AXIS, USE FLICK
GESTURE ON THE SURFACE

A direct interface allows users to directly change the UI elements presented to them. One of the popular implementations is in presenting 3-D objects. Three-dimensional transformations like moving, scaling, and rotating are key features that need continuous rendering of the 3-D objects with respect to *XYZ* axes. Direct interaction provides the best user experience in this case for moving and rotating the object.

Best Practices and Design Guidelines

- Have intuitive interaction—user should be able to touch and start interacting
- Use for application with multiple objects and shapes
- Use simple and familiar interactions for direct manipulation, such as drag for moving
- Have continuous representation of object on every movement
- Allow global interactions defined to manipulate the object as a whole
- Use specific interactions on the surface of the object for ad-hoc action
- Always allow user to reset and go back to the last position

(+) See also **3-D User Interface** on page 42 and **Gesture-Based User Interface** on page 71.

Rubik's Cube by CubeAssembler.com

The Rubik's Cube implementation is a simple example of a direct interface. It uses a combination of traditional UI components and menus along with a direct interface to the Rubik's Cube. The cube can be manipulated by applying flick gestures directly on the surface in a particular direction. There are global gestures for rotating the cube on the *X*- or *Y*- axis.

3-D IMPLEMENTATION OF RUBIK'S CUBE WITH DIRECT INTERFACE

DRAG OUTSIDE TO ROTATE THE CUBE

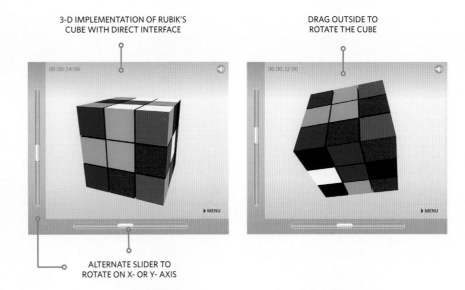

ALTERNATE SLIDER TO ROTATE ON X- OR Y- AXIS

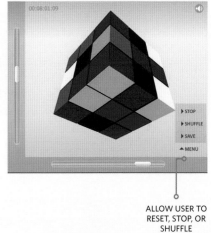

DRAG ON THE SURFACE TO MANIPULATE THAT SET OF CUBES

ALLOW USER TO RESET, STOP, OR SHUFFLE

3-D Interface

AN APPLICATION THAT ALLOWS THREE-DIMENSIONAL INTERACTIONS

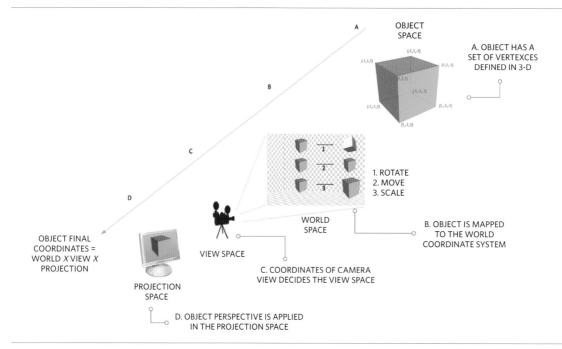

A. OBJECT HAS A SET OF VERTEXCES DEFINED IN 3-D

1. ROTATE
2. MOVE
3. SCALE

B. OBJECT IS MAPPED TO THE WORLD COORDINATE SYSTEM

OBJECT SPACE

WORLD SPACE

VIEW SPACE

C. COORDINATES OF CAMERA VIEW DECIDES THE VIEW SPACE

OBJECT FINAL COORDINATES = WORLD X VIEW X PROJECTION

PROJECTION SPACE

D. OBJECT PERSPECTIVE IS APPLIED IN THE PROJECTION SPACE

A 3-D interface is simulated in a 2-D flat screen and can be seen with bare eyes, unlike 3-D movies that must be experienced with special glasses. A 3-D interface assumes a three-dimensional virtual space where the object is mapped with respect to camera coordinates and projection to give a 3-D experience.

Best Practices and Design Guidelines
- Allow for predefined transformations based on requirement
- Provide intuitive user interface with mouse and keyboard
- Use zoom to get into multiple levels of the interface
- Use colors, gradients, and transparencies to differentiate between layers
- Always have quick help/legends for different interactions
- Keep an alternate (keyboard/mouse) method of interaction
- Allow for mistakes with undo/redo and reset options

(+) See also **Direct User Interface** on page 40 and **WIMP Interface** on page 14.

Windows Flip 3D

Windows Flip 3D is an intuitive 3-D interface introduced in Windows Vista. If you press the Windows button along with the tab key, you experience a 3-D interface that allows you to go through each of the open applications in three-dimensional cascading stacks. For each tab, the interface flips through open applications.

MICROSOFT WINDOWS FLIP 3D IN WINDOWS VISTA AND WINDOWS 7

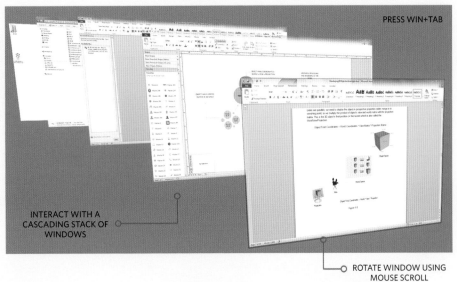

PRESS WIN+TAB

INTERACT WITH A CASCADING STACK OF WINDOWS

ROTATE WINDOW USING MOUSE SCROLL

THE 3-D RENDER PROCESS ON A COMPUTER SCREEN

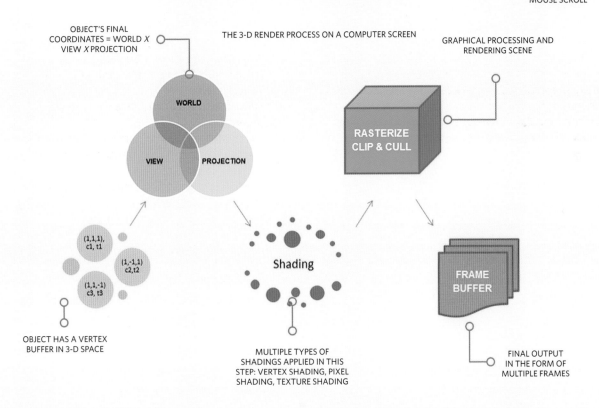

OBJECT'S FINAL COORDINATES = WORLD X VIEW X PROJECTION

WORLD

VIEW

PROJECTION

GRAPHICAL PROCESSING AND RENDERING SCENE

RASTERIZE CLIP & CULL

(1,1,1), c1, t1

(1,-1,1) c2,t2

(1,1,-1) c3, t3

Shading

FRAME BUFFER

OBJECT HAS A VERTEX BUFFER IN 3-D SPACE

MULTIPLE TYPES OF SHADINGS APPLIED IN THIS STEP: VERTEX SHADING, PIXEL SHADING, TEXTURE SHADING

FINAL OUTPUT IN THE FORM OF MULTIPLE FRAMES

Metro UI/Modern UI

A CONTENT-FOCUSED, TYPOGRAPHY-DRIVEN USER INTERFACE

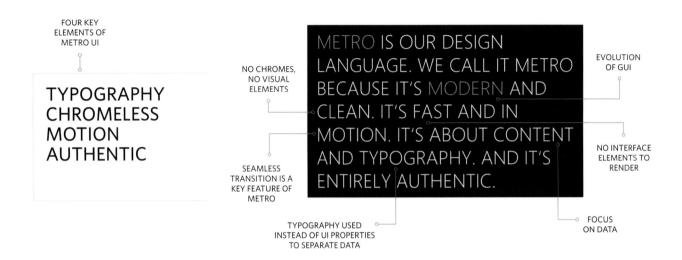

FOUR KEY ELEMENTS OF METRO UI

TYPOGRAPHY
CHROMELESS
MOTION
AUTHENTIC

NO CHROMES, NO VISUAL ELEMENTS

SEAMLESS TRANSITION IS A KEY FEATURE OF METRO

TYPOGRAPHY USED INSTEAD OF UI PROPERTIES TO SEPARATE DATA

EVOLUTION OF GUI

NO INTERFACE ELEMENTS TO RENDER

FOCUS ON DATA

METRO IS OUR DESIGN LANGUAGE. WE CALL IT METRO BECAUSE IT'S MODERN AND CLEAN. IT'S FAST AND IN MOTION. IT'S ABOUT CONTENT AND TYPOGRAPHY. AND IT'S ENTIRELY AUTHENTIC.

Metro UI is an interface introduced by Microsoft on Windows Phone 7 that uses content for navigation. Metro UI focuses on clean typography and avoids all forms of user interface chrome, such as borders, gradients, and shadows, unlike a GUI-based interface, which has UI elements with clear borders and visual properties.

Best Practices and Design Guidelines

- Have functional typography
    - Use the right balance of weight and positioning with white spaces
    - Create visual hierarchy to separate contents and navigation
- Allow live motion
    - Provide seamless, smooth animations for page transition to make it feel responsive
    - Use motion to give context for usability, extra dimension, and depth
    - Have consistent set of animations and improve perceived performance
- Create chromeless content
    - Focus on content without borders
    - Remove all notions of extra chrome in the UI
- Keep the UI authentically digital
    - Design for the form factor
    - Design for the high-resolution screen

(+) See also **Skeuomorphic Design UI** on page 46 and **Graphical User Interface (GUI)** on page 16.

VSLive New York 2012 Conference App

The VSLive app uses metro UI design principles to create a Windows phone app. The interface uses a panorama layout that has multiple screens showing event information, details on speakers, topics, locations, and schedules. The interface has only data and images of speakers to interact with and the views are borderless with seamless transitions. See http://tinyurl.com/VSLiveWP7App.

PANORAMA LAYOUT SHOWS DIFFERENT TYPES OF DATA IN ONE SEAMLESS SCREEN

CLEAR TYPOGRAPHY BRINGS FOCUS ON DATA

PAGES WITHOUT BORDERS OR VISUAL PROPERTIES

LEFT-RIGHT SWIPE GESTURE ALLOWS USER TO NAVIGATE BETWEEN TYPES OF INFORMATION

NO USER INTERFACE ELEMENTS— TAP THE DATA TO INTERACT

CLICK ON THE DATA TO CHECK DETAILS

TILES FOR GROUPING CATEGORIES

Skeuomorphic Design/Faux Real UI

AN INTERFACE DESIGNED TO LOOK AND BEHAVE LIKE REAL-LIFE OBJECTS

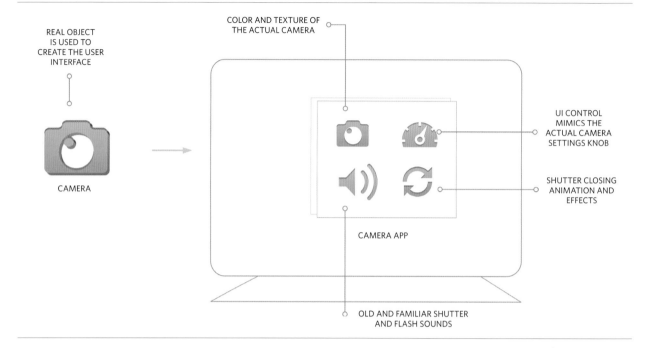

REAL OBJECT
IS USED TO
CREATE THE USER
INTERFACE

CAMERA

COLOR AND TEXTURE OF
THE ACTUAL CAMERA

UI CONTROL
MIMICS THE
ACTUAL CAMERA
SETTINGS KNOB

SHUTTER CLOSING
ANIMATION AND
EFFECTS

CAMERA APP

OLD AND FAMILIAR SHUTTER
AND FLASH SOUNDS

Skeuomorphic interface design blends the digital interface with physical object design and includes elements of design that serve no purpose in the artifact except familiarity. Skeuomorphic design (popularized by Apple) is an evolution of GUI for creating applications by using physical metaphors. For example, the virtual keyboard of the iPad has "bumps" in the F and J key, which are found in real keyboards to give a sensory feedback. Skeuomorphic design gives an old and familiar feeling to new related applications and tends to have a powerful emotional impact on users.

Best Practices and Design Guidelines

- Design based on metaphors that represent concrete, familiar ideas, and make them obvious
- Understand how the user interacts with similar real-life objects before creating an application
- Use similar look, color, sound, and animation effects from the real-world counterpart, such as designing a digital calendar based on a paper calendar
- Get help from a subject-matter expert for creating advanced professional applications
- Design the interface to help user understand the application

(+) See also **Graphical User Interface (GUI)** on page 16 and **Metro UI/Modern UI** on page 44.

iBooks App for iPad and iPhone

Apple iBooks app uses a skeuomorphic interface to create a familiar book like experience for eBooks. The app shows them in a realistic-looking wooden bookshelf.

The actual book, when "opened," shows page depth and mimics the page turn with animation and sound with touch gestures.

DESIGN TO MIMIC A REAL BOOKSHELF

BOOKS-AND-SHELF METAPHOR FOR GROUPING ELECTRONIC CONTENT

USE OF DEPTH AND SHADOWS FOR REALISTIC DISPLAY

COLORFUL, TACTILE COVERS FOR eBOOKS THAT DO NOT HAVE THEM GIVES A REALISTIC LOOK

PAGE DEPTH GIVES A FAMILIAR EXPERIENCE

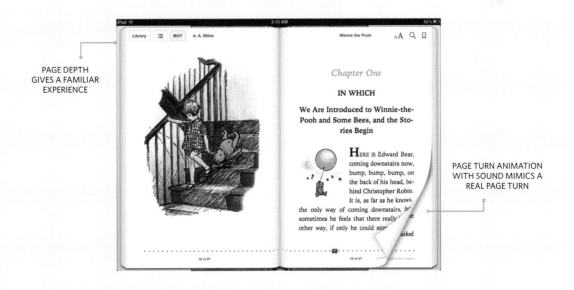

PAGE TURN ANIMATION WITH SOUND MIMICS A REAL PAGE TURN

21 Web User Interface (WUI)

AN APPLICATION INTERFACE ACCESSIBLE FROM A WEB BROWSER

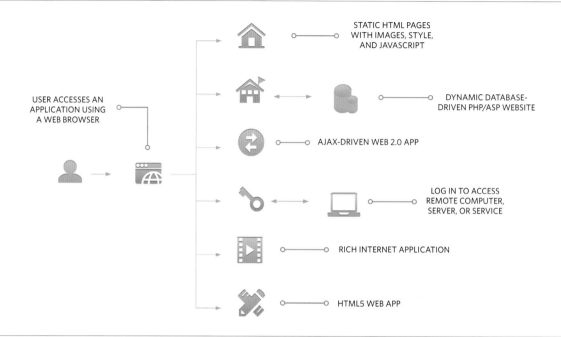

A web-based UI is an application made using HTML (Hypertext Markup Language) and is hosted in a local file system or a web server and accessed using a web browser. It can be a static website made of HTML, CSS, and JavaScript, or it can be a dynamic website developed in a server-based programming language like PHP/ASP or RIA technologies, or an HTML5-based app.

Best Practices and Design Guidelines
- Create a standard hierarchical structure with the homepage as the main page
- Divide each page's content into a grid layout with multiple rows and columns
- Keep consistency in the layout
- Break large content or complex tasks into multiple pages
- Limit navigation choices to six
- Use meaningful icons, colors, and letters to help users

- Give feedback to user action for long background tasks
- Use accessibility guidelines for content to allow maximum number of users
- Use attention-grabbing techniques sparingly

User Experience
- Use high-quality optimized pictures and graphics to inspire confidence
- Allow user to scan the content with blocks of information
- Have a task flow for applications
- Use prominent menus and links
- Avoid page refresh and constant animations
- Use precise and effective writing
- Strive for simplicity and use lots of white space
- Use aesthetic colors, visual cues, and icons to create a richer layout

(+) See also **Website** on page 52, **Homepage** on page 54, and **Accessible Web** on page 50.

FreshBooks is a cloud-based accounting application with a web interface. It uses a simple two-color theme, clear titles, white space, professional graphics, and familiar icons. The website has a simple yet effective flow to guide a user to the free trial.

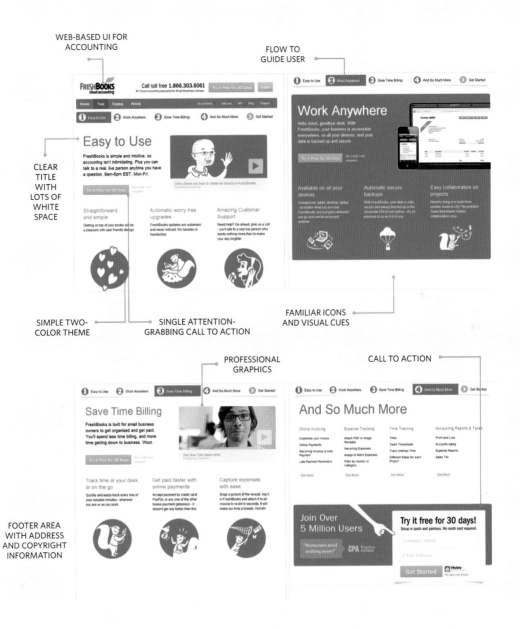

WEB-BASED UI FOR ACCOUNTING

FLOW TO GUIDE USER

CLEAR TITLE WITH LOTS OF WHITE SPACE

SIMPLE TWO-COLOR THEME

SINGLE ATTENTION-GRABBING CALL TO ACTION

FAMILIAR ICONS AND VISUAL CUES

PROFESSIONAL GRAPHICS

CALL TO ACTION

FOOTER AREA WITH ADDRESS AND COPYRIGHT INFORMATION

Accessible Web
A WEB INTERFACE THAT ACCOMMODATES USERS WITH DISABILITIES

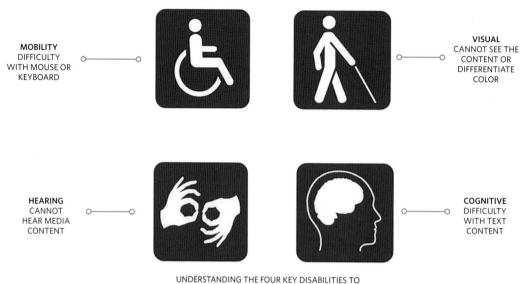

MOBILITY DIFFICULTY WITH MOUSE OR KEYBOARD

VISUAL CANNOT SEE THE CONTENT OR DIFFERENTIATE COLOR

HEARING CANNOT HEAR MEDIA CONTENT

COGNITIVE DIFFICULTY WITH TEXT CONTENT

UNDERSTANDING THE FOUR KEY DISABILITIES TO CREATE A TRULY ACCESSIBLE INTERFACE

An accessible interface gives maximum reach to your application's information, functionalities, and benefits. The four major disabilities that the accessible web interface addresses are visual, hearing, mobility (difficulty in using the mouse), and cognitive disabilities related to learning abilities.

Best Practices and Design Guidelines
- Design using semantically structured HTML for content, navigation, section, and articles
- Script presentation elements that change the visual content (e.g., bold, italics, color) in CSS
- Use "label" tag with "for" attribute for form elements "field set" and "legend" to group elements
- Use "summary," table heading "th" tag, and "scope" attribute when using HTML tables
- Always maintain a good contrast between foreground and background color
- Always make font size relative, never fixed
- Underline and use different colors for visited/nonvisited links

User Experience
- Make site structure clean and obvious; works best with two columns
- Use meaningful link text; avoid using "click here" or "more"
- Test navigation with keyboard tab for logical order and look for keyboard traps
- Use concise and meaningful content with simple words and short paragraphs
- Try putting most relevant content in the first three words of titles
- Use simple machine (screen reader) readable words like "home page," not "homepage"
- Always have one form in one page, and don't mix them with contents

(+) See also, **Accessible Touch** on page 170, **Website** on page 52, and **Homepage** on page 54.

Http://bbc.co.uk

The BBC news website is an accessible website. It also has information available in sign language. The accessibility section has a simple layout and is still graphically modern. It allows for custom font size, contrast options, keyboard access to all the links, and standard visual icons.

SIMPLE LAYOUT WITH MINIMUM LINKS IN THE TOP MENU

MAIN TOPIC ACCESSIBLE BY KEYBOARD TAB

CUSTOM FONT SIZE AND CHANGE COLOR CONTRAST OPTION

STANDARD VISUAL ICONS FOR EASY COMPREHENSION

SUBTITLE FOR MEDIA CONTENT

EASY ACCESS TO CONTENT HELP

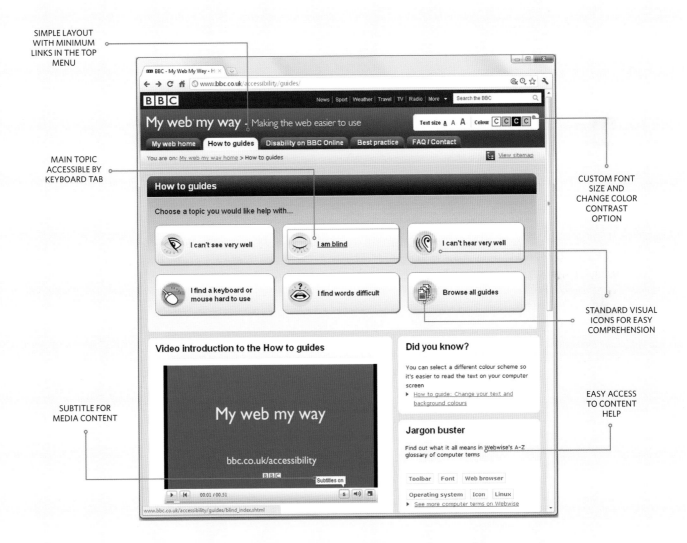

Website

A COLLECTION OF RELATED WEB PAGES, IMAGES, AND RESOURCES ACCESSED THROUGH A SINGLE WEB ADDRESS

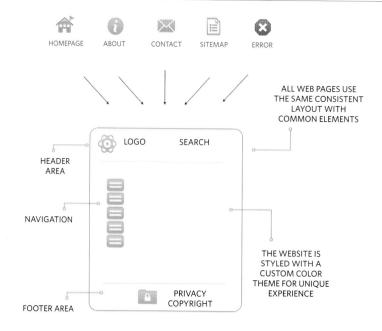

HOMEPAGE   ABOUT   CONTACT   SITEMAP   ERROR

ALL WEB PAGES USE THE SAME CONSISTENT LAYOUT WITH COMMON ELEMENTS

LOGO   SEARCH

HEADER AREA

NAVIGATION

THE WEBSITE IS STYLED WITH A CUSTOM COLOR THEME FOR UNIQUE EXPERIENCE

PRIVACY COPYRIGHT

FOOTER AREA

A website is an online presence for a company or an individual. It's made of web pages, which are text documents rendered as HTML in an Internet browser. A web page typically has associated images, media files, scripts, and style information that are embedded as links. The website is accessed through a web address called a URL (Uniform Resource Locator), which shows the homepage of the website.

Best Practices and Design Guidelines

Website design includes focusing on top tasks, having a content strategy, engaging visitors, and supporting as many browsers and platforms as possible.

- Keep the logo and company name prominent
- Use a maximum of three colors for the theme of the website using the logo colors
- Create informative page title, consistent site header, logo area, page footer, and navigation
- Balance content, graphics, and white space in the pages with good background contrast
- Clearly label and structure navigations
- Provide meaningful link labels, underlined with consistent color scheme for visited/nonvisited links

User Experience

- Focus on performance, with page-load times of fewer less than 10 seconds with dialup
- Allow for multiple browser support
- Engage customers using forums, suggestions, and feedback options
- "Search," if available, should be prominent and work for misspelled words
- Allow for text resizing and printing options
- Avoid pop-up windows, frames, and plug-ins
- Use accessible web guidelines

(+) See also **Homepage** on page 54, **Accessible Web** on page 50, and **Personal Web Page** on page 56.

Sumagency.com

Sumagency.com has a pleasing design. It uses three colors for the theme available in the logo. It has a clear navigation with lots of white space between text and graphics, and has a consistent header, footer, and logo area on all the pages.

HOMEPAGE WITH A GREETING

COMMON HEADER AREA WITH LOGO

ABOUT, CONTACT, AND NAVIGATON

A UNIQUE AESTHETIC COLOR THEME DISTINGUISHES THE WEBSITE

FOOTER AREA WITH ADDRESS AND COPYRIGHT INFORMATION

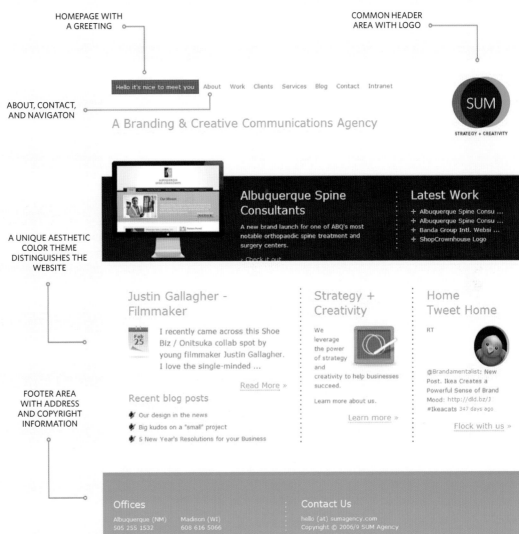

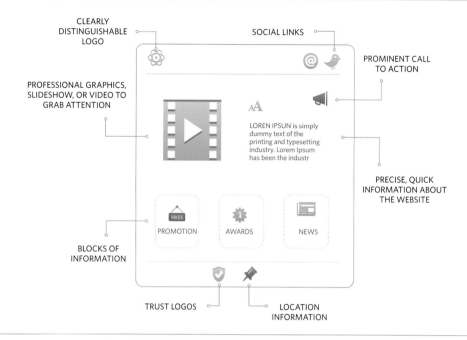

CLEARLY DISTINGUISHABLE LOGO

SOCIAL LINKS

PROMINENT CALL TO ACTION

PROFESSIONAL GRAPHICS, SLIDESHOW, OR VIDEO TO GRAB ATTENTION

LOREN IPSUN is simply dummy text of the printing and typesetting industry. Lorem Ipsum has been the industr

PRECISE, QUICK INFORMATION ABOUT THE WEBSITE

FREE
PROMOTION

AWARDS

NEWS

BLOCKS OF INFORMATION

TRUST LOGOS

LOCATION INFORMATION

A homepage is the default page that loads when the user visits the website. It is used to welcome visitors and to provide them with information and services. It acts as an entry page and an index for all of the site's content. available. It is meant to engage visitors to avail website information, products, and services.

Best Practices and Design Guidelines

- Use a unique design with visual hierarchy on the page
- Create user-centered design with emphasis on user-relevant content
- Use simple, clear, and understandable content, and avoid abbreviations, exclamations, and all caps
- Avoid the page scroll, and keep the important content above the scrollable area
- Avoid browser plug-in files like PDF and Flash

User Experience

- Clean aesthetic and minimalist design
- Quick access to contact support
- Avoid textured/tiled background
- Clearly visible contact information

(+) See also **Accessible Web** on page 50, **Website** on page 52, and **Blog** on page 60.

Zedo.com uses a clean and unique layout in which the theme of the website matches the logo. It has professional graphics and emphasized text for potential customers. The "Get Started" button clearly guides the customer to take the next step when they are ready.

SOCIAL
NETWORK
LINKS

CLEAR CALL
TO ACTION

CLEAR LOGO AND
DESCRIPTION

QUICK INFORMATION
ABOUT WEBSITE

PROFESSIONAL
GRAPHICS TO GRAB
ATTENTION

BLOCKS OF
INFORMATION

TRUST LOGOS

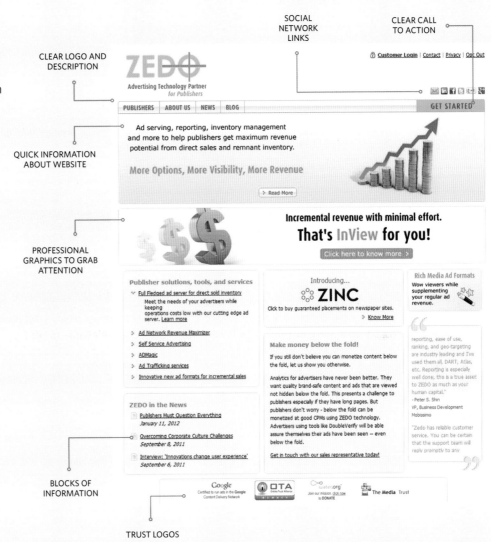

25 Personal Website

A WEBSITE DEDICATED FOR AN INDIVIDUAL

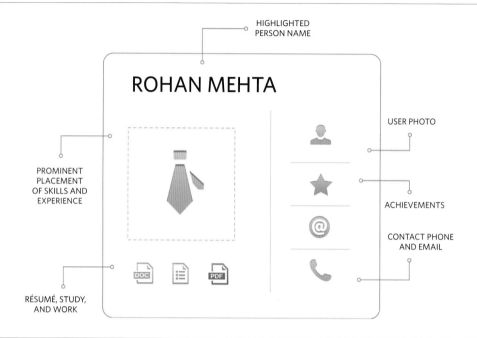

HIGHLIGHTED
PERSON NAME

ROHAN MEHTA

USER PHOTO

PROMINENT
PLACEMENT
OF SKILLS AND
EXPERIENCE

ACHIEVEMENTS

CONTACT PHONE
AND EMAIL

RÉSUMÉ, STUDY,
AND WORK

A personal website is a person's online identity. It can be a single web page, a static website, or a personal diary or blog. It can be an online portfolio for an artist with sample works or a simple website with résumé and work experience. It is also used as a professional way of presenting oneself and can be thought of as a glorified résumé on the web.

Best Practices and Design Guidelines

- Use the name as the logo—this is your personal brand
- Use the title of the page for quick information about you for search engines
- For résumé and other file downloads, use file names with no space
- Use legible fonts, headings, and bullets for formatting
- Add pictures and scanned certificates and awards for a personal touch
- Keep the content simple, clear, and decent

User Experience

- Make an impact by conveying your message on the first screen in the homepage
- Allow easy access to contact information
- Test all the links and file downloads
- Do not use frames, banner ads, or pop-up windows
- Do not post "under construction" pages; instead, don't include the link

(+) See also **Website** on page 52 and **Blog** on page 60

The personal website of Lakshmi Chava is professional and goal oriented. It is targeted to a potential hiring manager with sections for her résumé, study, and work experience. The navigation features a personal photo, certificates, and awards received. The phone number is prominently placed for a potential recruiter.

MAKE AN IMPACT HERE

CLEAR NAME TITLE WITHOUT A LOGO AND SIMPLE NAVIGATION

LINK TO RÉSUMÉ

CLEAN AND PROFESSIONAL DESIGN

LINK TO PROFESSIONAL NETWORK

PICTURE GIVES A PERSONAL TOUCH

CLEAR CONTACT INFORMATION

STANDOUT ACHIEVEMENTS

CONTENT PRIORITIZED BY RELEVANCE

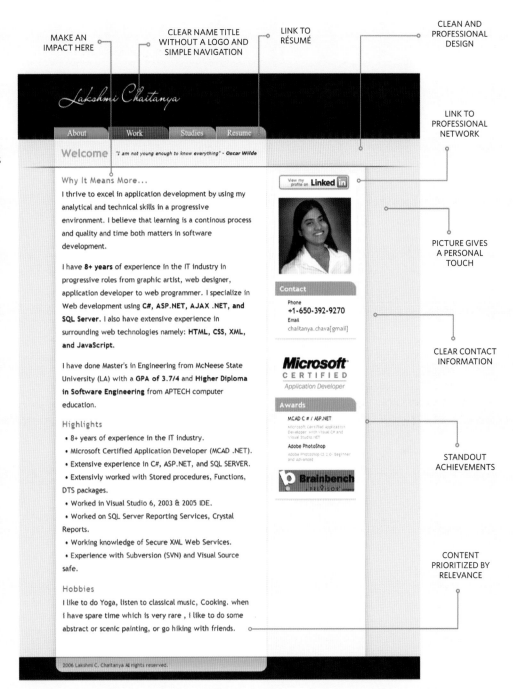

26

Single-Page Website

A WEBSITE THAT USES ONE WEB PAGE

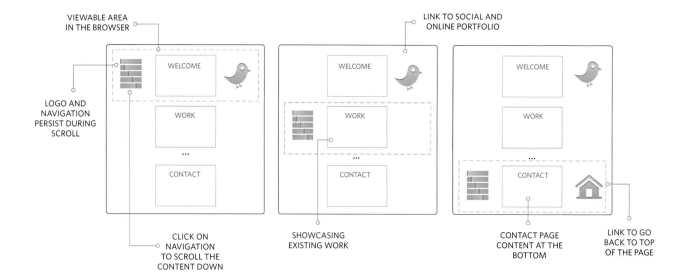

Single-page websites are the latest trend in web design. The site uses a long web page that scrolls vertically and the navigation links are anchored to different parts of the page. It's popular among portfolio and custom service provider websites.

Best Practices and Design Guidelines
- Popular sections in single-page website are
  - Top welcome section
  - Photo gallery
  - About section
  - Services and testimonials
- Use standard two or three color scheme with readable text
- Keep the logo position fixed along with navigation
- Have contact information with map on the page

Single-page websites are meant to give a better user experience.

User Experience
- Use slideshow if you need to show multiple images
- Always have a Go to Top button
- Use show/hide form/part of the content for better usability

(+) See also **Homepage** on page 54 and **Personal Website** on page 56.

Unicrow.com has a beautiful single-page design with a slideshow above the fold. It uses a single-color scheme and has a lot of white space, which makes the website very aesthetic and simple. It has content for about, services, work, and contact.

THE ICON AND THE NAVIGATION STAYS AT THE SAME PLACE, EVEN IF YOU SCROLL THE PAGE

ANCHOR LINKS TO THE CONTENT BELOW IN THE SAME PAGE

SIMPLE THEME WITH LOTS OF WHITE SPACE

SOCIAL LINKS

MULTIPLE IMAGES USE PICTURE SLIDESHOW

LINK TO WORK AND SERVICES OFFERED

THE WEB PAGE SCROLLS DOWN WHEN THE USER CLICKS ON THE NAVIGATION LINK

MORE THAN 1,000 WORDS WITH HIGHLIGHTED KEYWORDS PUT IT IN HIGH RANKING

CONTACT US FORM WITH ADDRESS INFORMATION

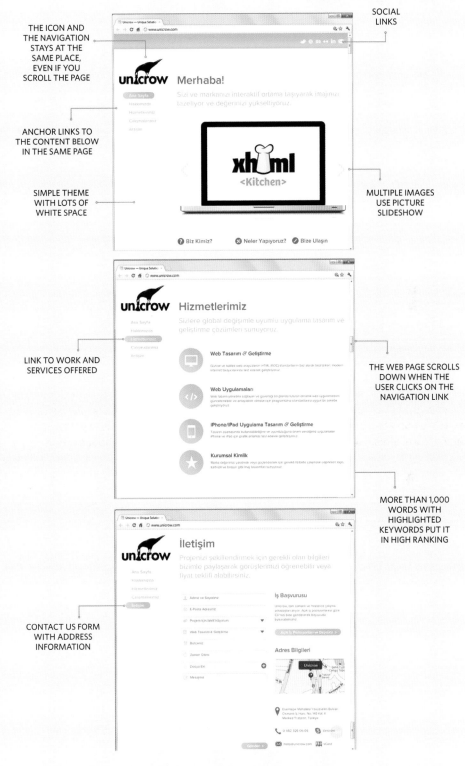

27

Blog

A DYNAMIC WEBSITE THAT FEATURES A PERSONAL DIARY OF A USER OR VOICE OF A GROUP

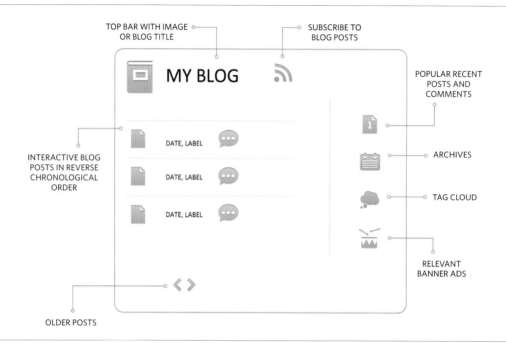

A blog consists of a user or a group of like-minded users who write about a certain topic or subject. Blogs are also effective for brand advertising. Blogs consist of user-generated content comprising posts that are updated frequently. A blog website features numerous web widgets, which allow the user to subscribe to blog posts and newsletters and to rate and share the blog post in the social network.

Best Practices and Design Guidelines
- Create custom attractive header and theme with gradients to give a unique identity
- Use familiar fonts and keep text clutter-free, formatted, and readable
- Use a light background and include a search box
- Use a layout with a maximum of 1,024 pixel width to support maximum number of computers
- Have one sidebar for calendar, archives, and recent posts
- Keep contact and subscription link prominent for immediate action by the visitor

User Experience
- Use optimized graphics in the homepage of the blog for quick loading
- Keep navigation simple and pages short for quick loading
- Limit banner ads and Flash-based rich Internet applications
- Keep an About page with author photo and biography for credibility
- Allow interactivity for immediate sharing and commenting

(+) See also **Personal Website** on page 56, **WordPress Theme** on page 64, and **Web Widget** on page 98.

Blog at Jagritisinha.com

Jagriti Sinha's blog uses WordPress, a popular platform for web publishing. The design is simple, featuring the blog title; a tagline with an image bar at the top sets the tone for the blog. Most of the real estate is used for the blog post on the left side, and the site has advanced widgets for sharing and commenting on the blog post.

NAME OF THE BLOG WITH NICE GRAPHICS

MOST RECENT BLOG POST

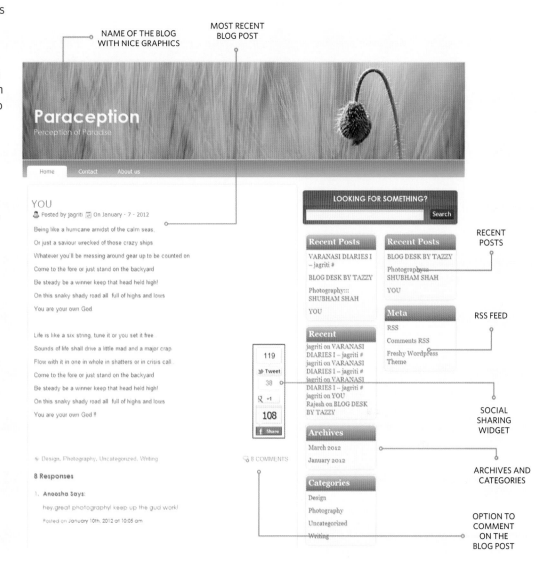

RECENT POSTS

RSS FEED

SOCIAL SHARING WIDGET

ARCHIVES AND CATEGORIES

OPTION TO COMMENT ON THE BLOG POST

28

Blogger Template

PRECONFIGURED CUSTOM LAYOUTS FOR BLOGS AT BLOGGER.COM

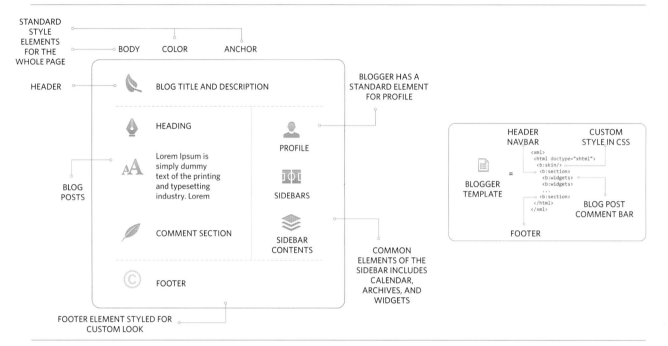

Blogger templates are predesigned to display your blog and post entries with a particular theme and layout and are used on Blogger.com. It gives a custom look to your blog and allows for further editing of styles. A Blogger.com template allows for a customizable look, provides choices for a multiple-column layout, and lets you change background color and images.

Best Practices and Design Guidelines

- Style all format elements, including headings, links, tables, bold, italics, etc
- Allow changing of color and fonts in template designer
- Host all the images used in the template on Blogger.com or a reliable public image hosting site
- Limiting the amount of branding in the footer is an acceptable practice
- Test your template for multiple browser and mobile compatibility

User expectations from a blogger template are both plug-n-play features and aesthetic looks.

User Experience

- Have professional graphics in the top header bar
- Have good color combinations (matching or contrasting) in the theme
- Choose a minimal number of colors in the theme
- Include social networking stickers for greater user experience
- Test your template at Blogger.com rigorously

(+) See also **Blog** on page 60 and **WordPress Theme** on page 64.

Widget-box.blogspot.com Theme

The Widget-box.blogspot.com uses a custom template for its blog with a simple design and color scheme. It uses very few colors overall, light colors for the background, black for content, and dark red for headings.

CUSTOM BACKGROUND IMAGE AND THEME USING THREE COLORS

HEADER AREA WITH TITLE AND DESCRIPTION

STYLED BLOG HEADING TO MATCH THE THEME

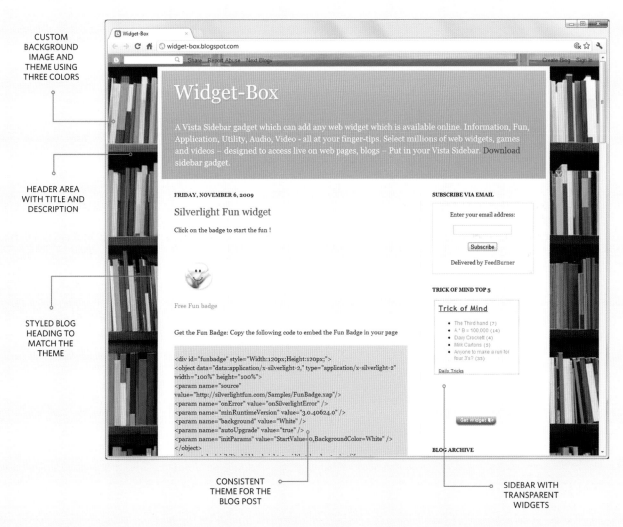

CONSISTENT THEME FOR THE BLOG POST

SIDEBAR WITH TRANSPARENT WIDGETS

29

WordPress Theme

TEMPLATE FOR LAYOUT AND STYLE FOR WORDPRESS BLOG PLATFORM

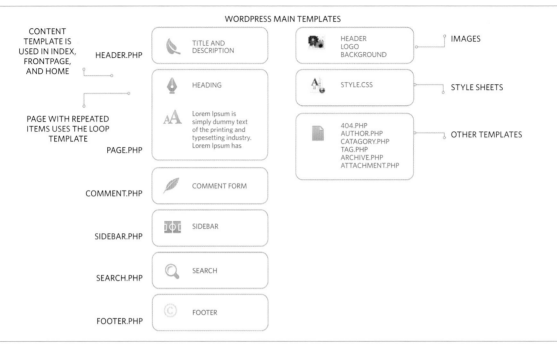

A collection of templates, style sheets, and images creates a unique GUI for a website based on WordPress (a popular content management system). The actual content is database driven and is unaffected by the theme. WordPress themes are assets of PHP files and allow you to change the basic structure, including page templates, mini posts, and numerous settings and customizations available in the theme.

Best Practices and Design Guidelines
- Start with a bare-bones theme with a two- or three-column layout
- Use a fluid layout, which adapts itself according to the browser size
- Allow change of header and background image with color options
- Use widgets, tag cloud, and RSS properly in the sidebar
- Allow ability to add visitor statistics widgets and banner ads easily
- Include SEO meta tags in header template

User expectations from a WordPress theme are aesthetic looks and full customizability.

User Experience
- Use two or three colors in the theme with readable fonts for content
- Allow internationalization and localization of themes with language attributes
- Use coding standard for HTML, CSS, and PHP for easy maintainability for developers
- Have your themes targeted for a particular type of website, such as education or photography

(+) See also **Blogger Template** on page 62 and **Blog** on page 60.

ElegantTheme.com's Nova Studio

The theme Nova Studio is an example of elegant design; it uses Helvetica for easy readability and two colors for the whole theme. The theme is completely customizable with the following features: multiple browser compatibility, advertisements, widget-ready sidebars, threaded comments with gravatars, localization support, and more.

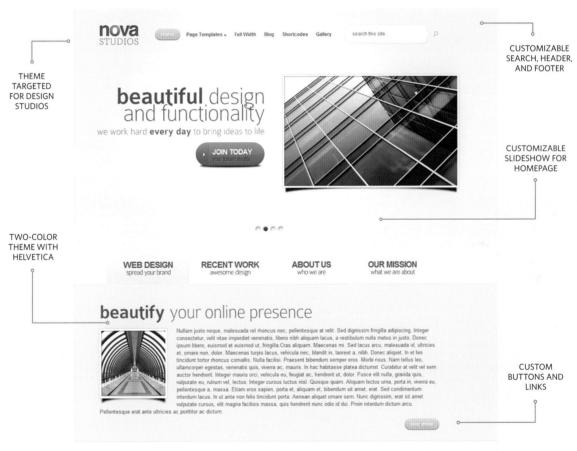

THEME TARGETED FOR DESIGN STUDIOS

TWO-COLOR THEME WITH HELVETICA

CUSTOMIZABLE SEARCH, HEADER, AND FOOTER

CUSTOMIZABLE SLIDESHOW FOR HOMEPAGE

CUSTOM BUTTONS AND LINKS

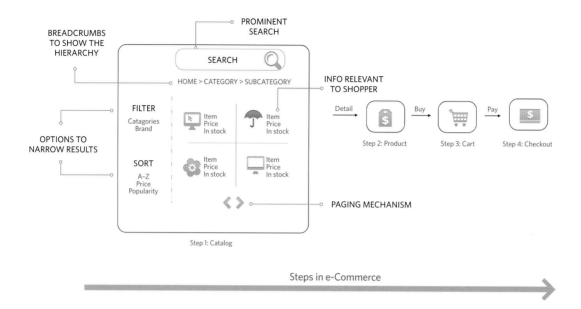

Step 1: Catalog

Steps in e-Commerce

A catalog is a visual list of products meant to help customers find a product to buy. It is also sometimes called a category or product listing page. A clearly organized list of products is key to a great e-commerce user experience. A catalog is the first step in e-commerce, where a user decides to buy a product after browsing, sorting, and filtering through multiple items.

The design of the product listing page should help users find the product.

Best Practices and Design Guidelines

- Create clean and aesthetic gallery listing (grid view) or vertical listing (list view) of products
- Provide a user-friendly and intelligent search with option for keywords, model number, category, and so on
- Classify items in terms of category and brand to further browse
- Make a consistent display format with list view, grid view (4×8), and large grid view (2×4)
- Help users shop by providing information about product, thumbnails, price, and availability

User Experience

- Fast response time is desirable, so keep the default list small; 24 for low bandwidth
- Keep browse and search results similar for less confusing experience
- Allow user to narrow the search or search within search
- Clean, uncluttered, and professional layout inspires trust and confidence in shoppers

(+) See also **Product Page Detail** on page 68 and **Shopping Cart** on page 70.

Olive and Myrtle

The catalog for Olive and Myrtle shows an aesthetic layout with a simple design. It allows users to increase the number of products on the page. It uses a lot of white space that is much easier on the eyes.

PROMINENT PLACEMENT OF SEARCH

CUSTOM NUMBER OF RESULTS

BREADCRUMBS SHOWING YOUR LOCATION FROM HOME

CATEGORIES TO FILTER THE RESULTS

SORT RESULTS OPTION

CLEAN AND CONSISTENT LAYOUT

RELEVANT INFORMATION WITH ADD TO CART OPTION

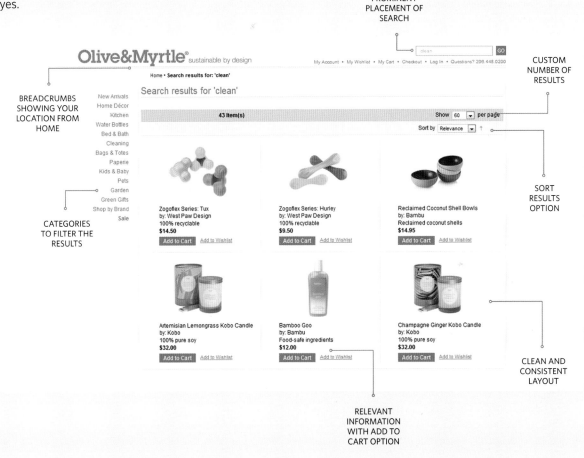

31 Product Page

A SINGLE, DETAILED INFORMATION PAGE FOR A PRODUCT

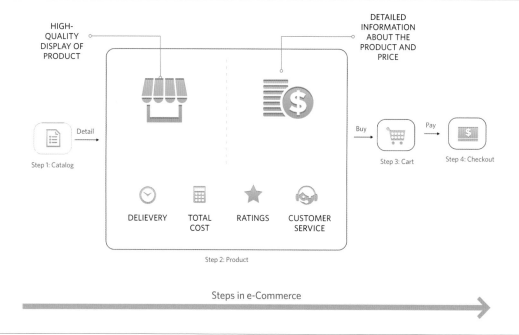

Steps in e-Commerce

A product page is an information-rich page meant to help shoppers decide on buying a product. It is meant to be a single page with all the information required, including images, specifications, size, color, discounts, shipping cost, customization options, and related media on the product.

Best Practices and Design Guidelines

- Use a two-column layout with pictures on the left and other information on the right
- Include everything on a single page so users don't waste time looking back and forth
- Keep bulleted list of information for quick access
- Use breadcrumbs navigation to go back to product category to choose another product
- Add to Cart button should be prominent to encourage shopping

User Experience

- Product name should be displayed prominently with high-quality product photos
- Include multiple photos at different angles for better visibility
- Scroll down or show information in tabs on the same page and avoid page reload
- Use "Add to Cart" button instead of "Buy" button
- User-generated content, including ratings and reviews, inspires trust

(+) See also **Catalog** on page 66 and **Shopping Cart** on page 70.

Land's End Product Page

The product detail page at Land's End is clutter-free and beautiful. Multiple high-quality images at different angles give users a chance to "feel" the actual product. Quick options for color and size instantly help users take the next step.

OPTION FOR CUSTOM FIT AND COLOR

MULTIPLE HIGH-QUALITY PICTURE OF THE PRODUCT

CLEAN AND AESTHETIC TWO-COLUMN LAYOUT WITH A SIDEBAR

INTERACTIVE "ADD TO CART" BUTTON

CROSS PROMOTING SIMILAR RELATED ITEMS

CONTACT FOR CUSTOMER SERVICE

RATING WITH DETAILED CUSTOMER REVIEWS

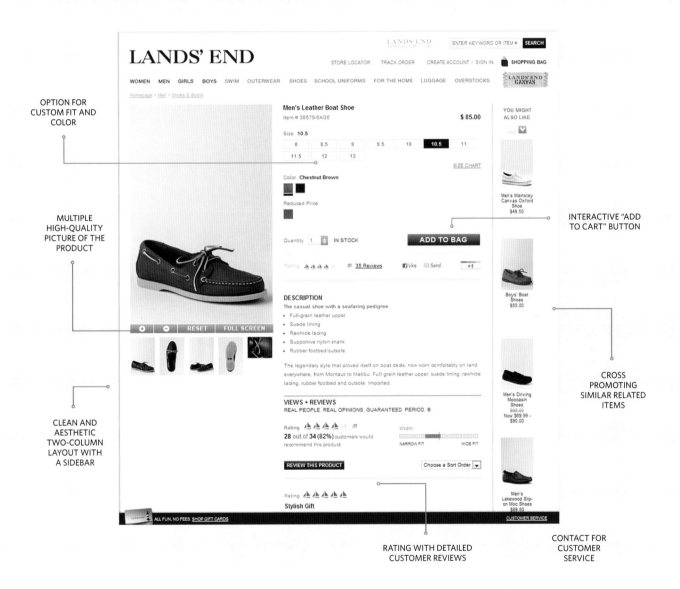

A SHOPPING CART ALLOWS CUSTOMERS TO PURCHASE MORE THAN ONE ITEM ONLINE

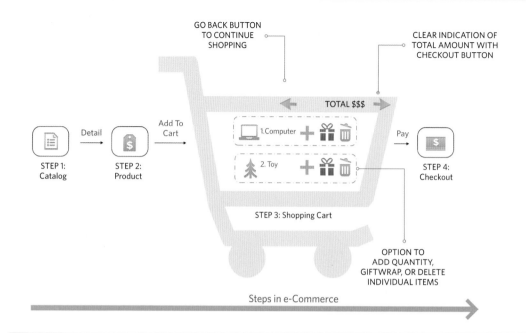

A shopping cart application allows you to easily add multiple items to the cart and check the final price, including shipping, taxes, and any other costs, before finalizing the purchase. The shopping cart is the third step in e-commerce.

Best Practices and Design Guidelines
- Use a prominent, aesthetically pleasing Checkout button to encourage buying
- Use website color scheme in the shopping cart with visible top navigation bar
- Create a clear shopping cart summary with all the upfront costs
- Show clickable item with thumbnail in the cart for review
- Use empty cart for shopping instructions for first-time visitors

User Experience
- Allow simple ways to update or remove quantity in the cart
- Have clean and distraction-free shopping cart page
- Inform user about enabled security for assurance
- Include a quick preview while browsing for more items in the top-right corner of the page

(+) See also **Catalog** on page 66, **Product Page** on page 68, and **Checkout** on page 72.

Shopping Carts at Walmart and Amazon

The shopping cart interface at Walmart.com is easy to use and has a consistent look and feel with the top navigation bar in place. It also gives an updated summary any time the user changes the items in the cart.

Amazon.com's shopping cart is a bit more sophisticated, displaying users' recently viewed history and "Saved per actual screen for Later," giving users more purchasing options based on recent activity.

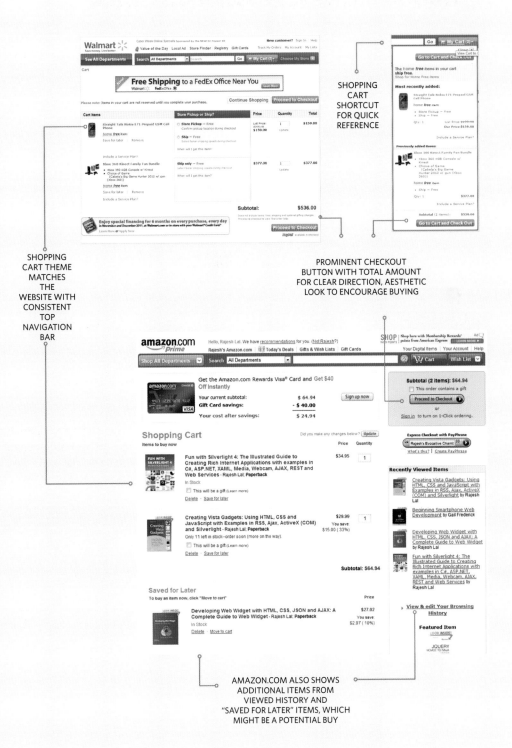

SHOPPING CART SHORTCUT FOR QUICK REFERENCE

SHOPPING CART THEME MATCHES THE WEBSITE WITH CONSISTENT TOP NAVIGATION BAR

PROMINENT CHECKOUT BUTTON WITH TOTAL AMOUNT FOR CLEAR DIRECTION, AESTHETIC LOOK TO ENCOURAGE BUYING

AMAZON.COM ALSO SHOWS ADDITIONAL ITEMS FROM VIEWED HISTORY AND "SAVED FOR LATER" ITEMS, WHICH MIGHT BE A POTENTIAL BUY

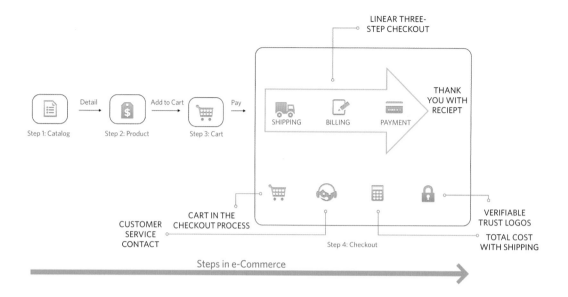

Steps in e-Commerce

This is the final step in e-commerce where the sale transaction occurs. In this step, the buyer pays for the item in the shopping cart using an online payment method like a credit card and gets a receipt. Checkout is a three-step process: obtaining shipping, billing, and online payment information.

Best Practices and Design Guidelines

- Use a progress indicator to show where user is in checkout process
- Use distraction- and links-free navigation during checkout process, also known as enclosed checkout
- Keep the existing shopping cart visible for review
- Provide optional Log in to Account step for existing customers
- Use Guest Checkout or better Start Checkout option for new customers
- Provide order summary page with Buy button to charge the buyer

User Experience

- Online chat helps user with any immediate concerns
- Fewer steps with default options
- For one-time buying service, one-page checkout process is better
- Address buyer's concerns about security, delivery, return, and customer service

(+) See also **Catalog** on page 66, **Product Page** on page 68, and **Shopping Cart** on page 70.

Land's End Checkout Process

A three-step process on a single page gives a great user experience. The always visible shopping cart gives reassurance to the buyer. Use of early shipping calculation, and Start Checkout for first-time customers are great features.

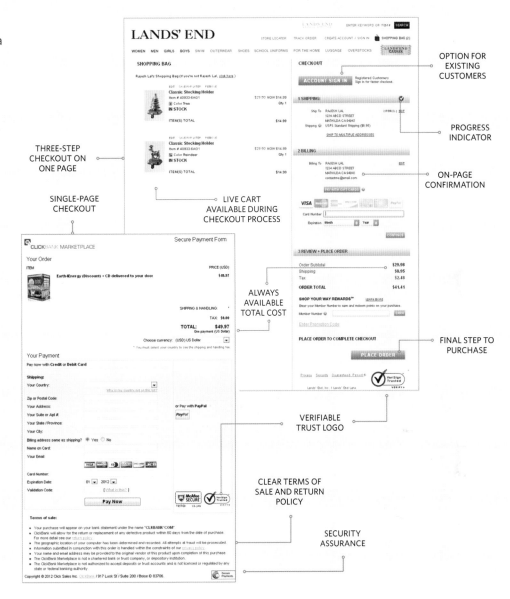

OPTION FOR EXISTING CUSTOMERS

PROGRESS INDICATOR

ON-PAGE CONFIRMATION

THREE-STEP CHECKOUT ON ONE PAGE

SINGLE-PAGE CHECKOUT

LIVE CART AVAILABLE DURING CHECKOUT PROCESS

ALWAYS AVAILABLE TOTAL COST

FINAL STEP TO PURCHASE

VERIFIABLE TRUST LOGO

CLEAR TERMS OF SALE AND RETURN POLICY

SECURITY ASSURANCE

34 User Account/Registration

THE PROCESS OF REGISTERING WITH A WEBSITE TO AVAIL PERSONALIZED SERVICES

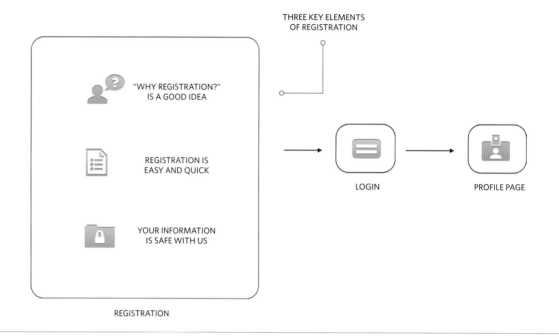

THREE KEY ELEMENTS
OF REGISTRATION

"WHY REGISTRATION?"
IS A GOOD IDEA

REGISTRATION IS
EASY AND QUICK

YOUR INFORMATION
IS SAFE WITH US

LOGIN

PROFILE PAGE

REGISTRATION

Account creation is the first step in creating a potential customer base. It allows companies to create a database of users and provides a medium for promotion. Registration helps visitors identify themselves to the online service and saves users time. An account can be free for a basic newsletter or paid for premium features.

Best Practices and Design Guidelines
- Use a one-page registration form for easy account creation
- Make benefits of registration clear on the registration page
- Keep registration fields to a bare minimum
- Provide quick validation and assistance to avoid user mistyping or losing data
- Have a clear privacy policy

User Experience
- Have descriptive inline help for each registration field with examples of valid entries
- Email address or having unique user name is easier
- If using email address as login name, make it clear that the password field is a new password users have to create (it is not user's existing email password)
- Keep clear distinction between login for existing customer and registration for new customer
- Clearly explain how registration will help with faster shopping and consider offering an incentive

(+) See also **Login** on page 76, **WordPress Theme** on page 64, and **User Profile** on page 78.

TrickofMind.com, a Puzzle-Sharing Website

TrickofMind.com allows users to register to post their own puzzles and comment on existing puzzles. It doesn't ask the user to enter password information; rather, the site emails a temporary password to the email address.

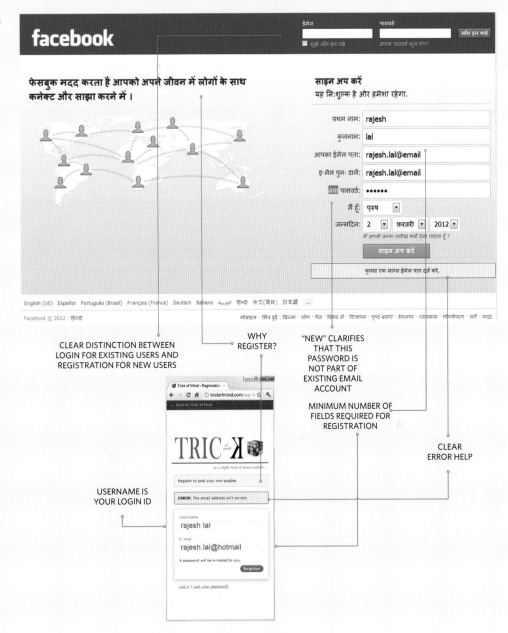

CLEAR DISTINCTION BETWEEN LOGIN FOR EXISTING USERS AND REGISTRATION FOR NEW USERS

WHY REGISTER?

"NEW" CLARIFIES THAT THIS PASSWORD IS NOT PART OF EXISTING EMAIL ACCOUNT

MINIMUM NUMBER OF FIELDS REQUIRED FOR REGISTRATION

CLEAR ERROR HELP

USERNAME IS YOUR LOGIN ID

A SECURITY MECHANISM TO IDENTIFY USERS ONLINE

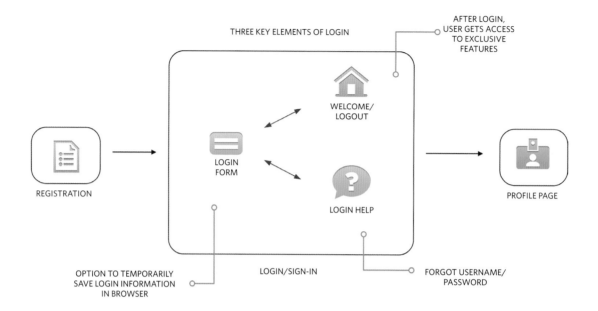

THREE KEY ELEMENTS OF LOGIN

AFTER LOGIN, USER GETS ACCESS TO EXCLUSIVE FEATURES

WELCOME/ LOGOUT

REGISTRATION

LOGIN FORM

LOGIN HELP

PROFILE PAGE

OPTION TO TEMPORARILY SAVE LOGIN INFORMATION IN BROWSER

LOGIN/SIGN-IN

FORGOT USERNAME/ PASSWORD

The login process allows a visitor to go through an authentication mechanism using a combination of a user name and password. The user name uniquely identifies the user, and the password authorizes the validity and access level of the account. Users are then redirected to their account page.

Best Practices and Design Guidelines

- Keep the logo of the website in both login form and forgot password form
- After login, greet the user with his name, giving him logout option
- Clear validation messages on the same page using multiple cues such as color, text, etc
- Use Captcha control, which asks user to read text from an image to confirm user
- Login help form for user to retrieve username/ password

User Experience

- Clear error messages on whether the login/password was wrong or if the account is locked
- Quick password reset option if the user forgot the password
- Include security best practices or phishing alert in the login screen
- Have a login form on the homepage
- Make the login form accessible from keyboard only and ensure logical tab order

+ See also **User Account/Registration** on page 74 and **User Profile** on page 78.

The login form is simple and without any other content. It has a link to registration and also provides a help link, "Lost Your Password," to retrieve a new password. The login help form has clear instructions to retrieve a password.

CLEAR
ERROR HELP

LINK TO
REGISTER

LOGIN HELP

LOGIN HELP
WITH CLEAR
INSTRUCTIONS

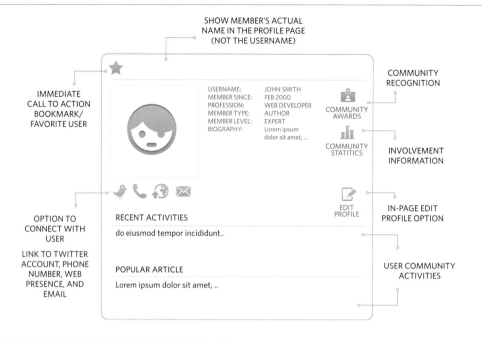

SHOW MEMBER'S ACTUAL NAME IN THE PROFILE PAGE (NOT THE USERNAME)

IMMEDIATE CALL TO ACTION BOOKMARK/ FAVORITE USER

COMMUNITY RECOGNITION

USERNAME: JOHN SMITH
MEMBER SINCE: FEB 2000
PROFESSION: WEB DEVELOPER
MEMBER TYPE: AUTHOR
MEMBER LEVEL: EXPERT
BIOGRAPHY: Lorem ipsum dolor sit amet, ...

COMMUNITY AWARDS

COMMUNITY STATITICS

INVOLVEMENT INFORMATION

EDIT PROFILE

IN-PAGE EDIT PROFILE OPTION

OPTION TO CONNECT WITH USER

LINK TO TWITTER ACCOUNT, PHONE NUMBER, WEB PRESENCE, AND EMAIL

RECENT ACTIVITIES

do eiusmod tempor incididunt..

POPULAR ARTICLE

Lorem ipsum dolor sit amet, ..

USER COMMUNITY ACTIVITIES

A user profile consists of a set of personal data, including name/pseudonym, picture/avatars, short biography, profession, hobbies, and other interests, which collectively represent the user in the online community. The user profile displays all user information along with the community activities.

Best Practices and Design Guidelines

- Use one-page layout for complete user information
- Place user's picture/avatar and community statistics at the top of the page
- Provide in-page edit option for users to change their profile
- Clear call to action for bookmark, contact, and connect with the user

User Experience

- Display member's real name along with the username
- Allow customization with HTML presentation elements to help user organize contents
- Accommodate beginning users to advanced users
- Have default avatar for all joining users

(+) See also **Login** on page 76, **User Account/Registration** on page 74, and **Online Forums** on page 80.

CodeProject.com and Foursquare

CodeProject.com has a detailed profile page with complete information about the user and her community activities. The Foursquare profile page is much simpler but has social badges, which encourage user activities on the website.

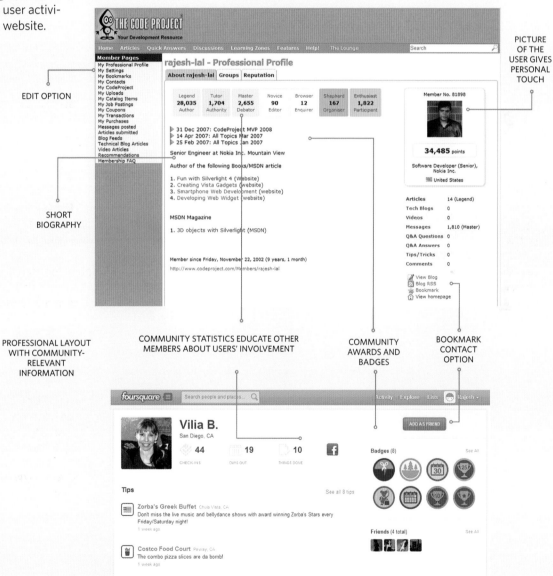

EDIT OPTION

SHORT
BIOGRAPHY

PROFESSIONAL LAYOUT
WITH COMMUNITY-
RELEVANT
INFORMATION

COMMUNITY STATISTICS EDUCATE OTHER
MEMBERS ABOUT USERS' INVOLVEMENT

COMMUNITY
AWARDS AND
BADGES

BOOKMARK
CONTACT
OPTION

PICTURE
OF THE
USER GIVES
PERSONAL
TOUCH

37

Online Forums

WEBSITE WHERE USERS CAN DISCUSS ISSUES, ASK QUESTIONS, AND INTERACT WITH EACH OTHER

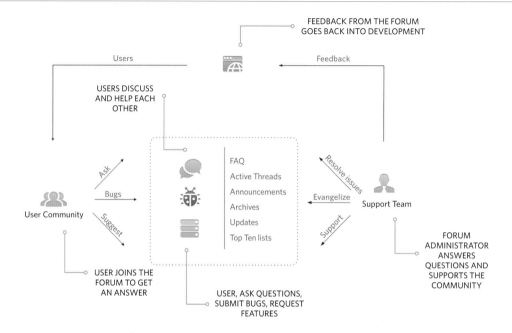

Online forums, also known as bulletin/message boards, are online places where users with similar interests come together to discuss features, bugs, and enhancements related to a product or service. Discussion forums are used to support user communities and have become a part of software/service offerings.

Best Practices and Design Guidelines
- Allow users to easily participate in the discussion with a simple email login process or as a guest
- Allow most active thread to filter to the top of the archived thread list
- Group topics into relevant, easy-to-find categories
- Allow full-featured text input with emoticons for richer interaction
- Show statistics for the number of users registered, online, and active

User Experience
- Show statistics for each thread based on activity
- Have section to contact the administrator
- Keep the forum real time and dynamic

(+) See also **Chat Room** on page 35, **Knowledgebase** on page 88, and **User Profile** on page 78.

Interviewinfo.net

Interviewinfo.net is an online forum for job seekers and offers free resources. The forum page shows how the questions are categorized into multiple headings and subheadings with the number of threads, posts, etc. The right-hand navigation bar also archives all the active threads, unanswered threads, and active users.

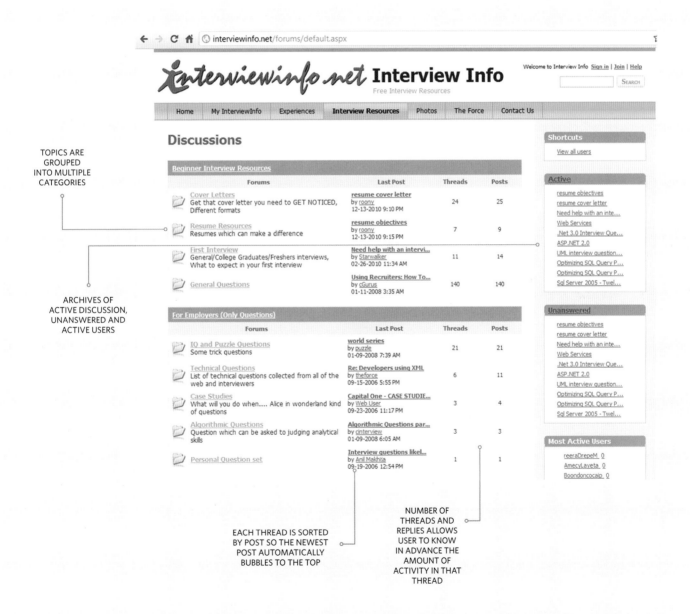

TOPICS ARE GROUPED INTO MULTIPLE CATEGORIES

ARCHIVES OF ACTIVE DISCUSSION, UNANSWERED AND ACTIVE USERS

EACH THREAD IS SORTED BY POST SO THE NEWEST POST AUTOMATICALLY BUBBLES TO THE TOP

NUMBER OF THREADS AND REPLIES ALLOWS USER TO KNOW IN ADVANCE THE AMOUNT OF ACTIVITY IN THAT THREAD

38

Comment Thread

LOGICAL GROUPING OF COMMENTS IN A CONVERSATION

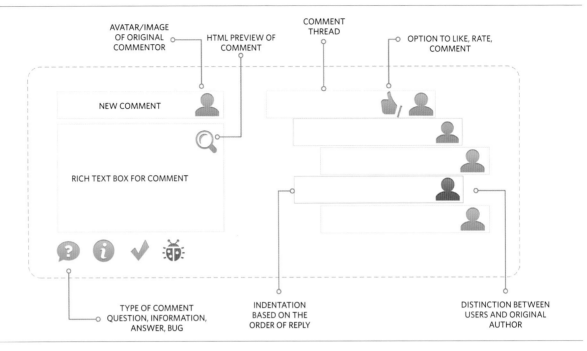

A comment thread is a set of comments grouped hierarchically based on a topic for easy access later. It is ordered in descending order and indented logically so as to show the newest comment at the top and the most-recent reply in the comment thread.

Best Practices and Design Guidelines

- Include an avatar/icon for users
- Have a rich theme to keep users engaged
- Keep an interactive comment thread with option to minimize all content
- Use different background colors to separate different user comments
- Use number count for replies to individual comment thread
- Add comment reply page with rich text options

User Experience

- Optimize the display to show maximum number of comments
- Have an option for quick reply
- Option to interact, rate, and add like to individual comments and replies
- Have standard icons for different types of comments, such as news, fun, and questions
- Instead of date/time, show how long ago in terms of minutes and hours the comment was made

(+) See also **Online Forums** on page 80 and **Chat Room** on page 35.

CodeProject.com Lounge

This is a developer forum that features rich comment threads. It allows a user to add comments of different types to an existing article and reply to them.

OPTION TO ADD NEW COMMENT

CONSISTENT THEME OF WEBSITE

COLLAPSIBLE COMMENT THREAD

TYPE OF MESSAGE, QUESTION, OR COMMENT

COMMENT REPLIES ARE GROUPED UNDER THAT COMMENT

DIFFERENT TYPES OF USERS HAVE DIFFERENT ICON AVATARS

THE WEB SERVICE SETS PARAMETER DIRECTLY ON THE WEB URL

DIFFERENT TYPES OF MESSAGES

RICH TEXT MESSAGE INPUT WITH LIST OF EMOTICONS

HTML LIVE PREVIEW OF THE MESSAGE

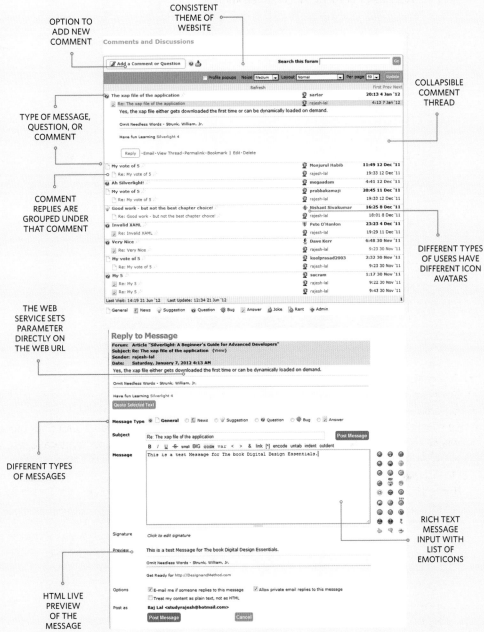

39

Sitemap

A WEB PAGE THAT SHOWS AN OVERALL STRUCTURE AND HIERARCHY OF A WEBSITE

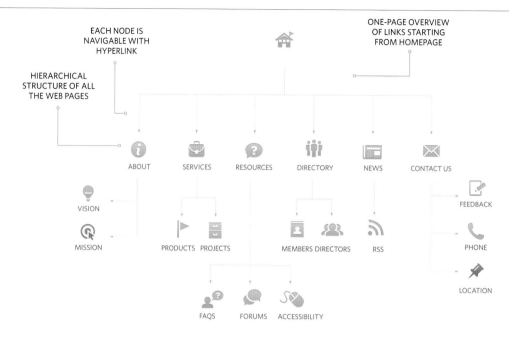

A sitemap is a well-structured, navigational map of all the pages available on the website, with hyperlinks for easy access. It is meant for both users and search engines for indexing purposes. It also lists sections on the website that are dynamically generated and not accessible from the homepage.

Best Practices and Design Guidelines
- Keep sitemap link on the website navigation
- Follow standard structures for creating a sitemap
   - Hierarchical tree structure—links starting from the homepage
   - Categorical—blocks of simple lists of sections with titles and links
   - Categorical with multiple levels—blocks of lists with three level subcategories
   - Graphical—flowchart-like structure with subnodes and links
- Use a simple static HTML page for sitemap
- Use descriptive and relevant keyword-rich anchor text
- Use the website header and footer for consistency
- Follow accessible content guidelines

User Experience
- Have user-friendly and logical categorization to helps users find things
- Use minimal graphics and avoid animations, ads, and RIAs on the page
- Use it in the error 404 page
- Avoid very large page for sitemap
- If you are using sitemap in the footer, keep the length to one-third of the page

(+) See also **Accessible Web** on page 50, **Homepage** on page 54, and **Resource Center/Help Center** on page 86.

Usability.com.au and Wblrd.sk.ca Sitemaps

Usability.com's website uses a hierarchical tree-like structure for its sitemap. It has a simple theme with no graphics and banner ads and features an accessibility tool. Wblrd's sitemap uses a categorical block structure. It's a simple text-based one-page sitemap.

LOGO AND TOP BAR CONSISTENT WITH THE WEBSITE

HIERARCHICAL LIST

LIST OF ALL SUBCATEGORY PAGES FOR EASY ACCESS TO SITE VISITOR

SIMPLE THEME WITH NO GRAPHICS AND BANNER ADS

ACCESSIBLE TEXT-BASED PAGE

CATEGORICAL BLOCKS OF SIMPLE LISTS

ONE-PAGE VIEW WITH ACCESSIBLE TEXT

SITEMAP LINK IN THE FOOTER

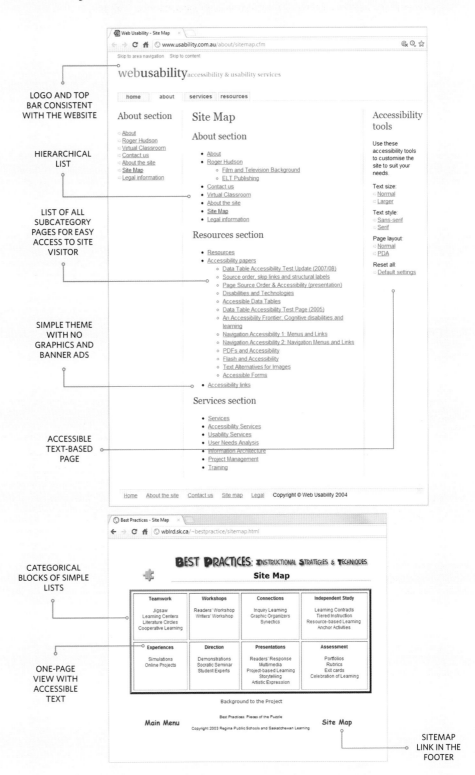

40

Resource Center/Help Center

A REFERENCE SECTION OF THE WEBSITE WITH COMPREHENSIVE INFORMATION FOR VISITORS

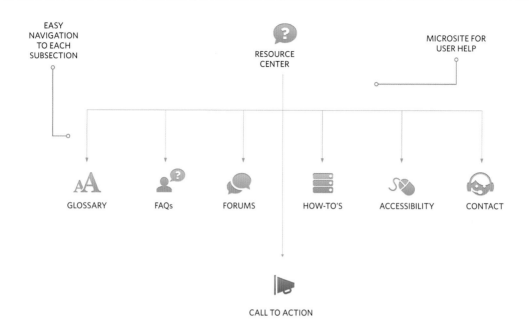

Resource centers are sections of websites to educate visitors about the company, product, or services. It engages users with frequently asked questions, quick information, a glossary, and useful downloads. It is a great tool to increase brand awareness and mindshare.

Best Practices and Design Guidelines
- Have a simple layout with minimal graphics, except for icons or screenshots
- Make it dynamic with regularly updated information
- Have a call to action
- Use accessible titles and link guidelines for FAQ and glossary pages
- Have a forum for user interaction
- Provide accessibility guide and contact information for further queries

User Experience
- Keep the simple layout for the resource center consistent with all subsections
- Use an easy-to-navigate and comprehensive glossary
- Use one-page FAQs and one-page glossary
- Do not use banner ads
- For the FAQs page, keep a list of questions at the top with anchor links to answers

(+) See also **Knowledgebase** on page 88, **Website** on page 52, and **Homepage** on page 54.

Gbci.org and Ameritas Group Resource Centers

Gbci.org has a simple layout for its resource section and features information in the form of handbooks, guides, glossaries, and other downloads. Ameritas Group has a unique resource center tailored for their users, which is different for providers and benefits administrators. The layout is minimal and free of any distraction, with no banner ads.

A-Z INDEX WITH ANCHORS TO DEFINITIONS

SIMPLE LAYOUT

FAQS PAGE WITH LIST OF QUESTIONS WITH ANCHORS TO ANSWERs

SIMPLE NAVIGATION TO GO BACK TO RESOURCE CENTER

GLOSSARY, FAQS AND PRODUCT INFORMATION

MINIMAL GRAPHICS AND NO AD BANNERS

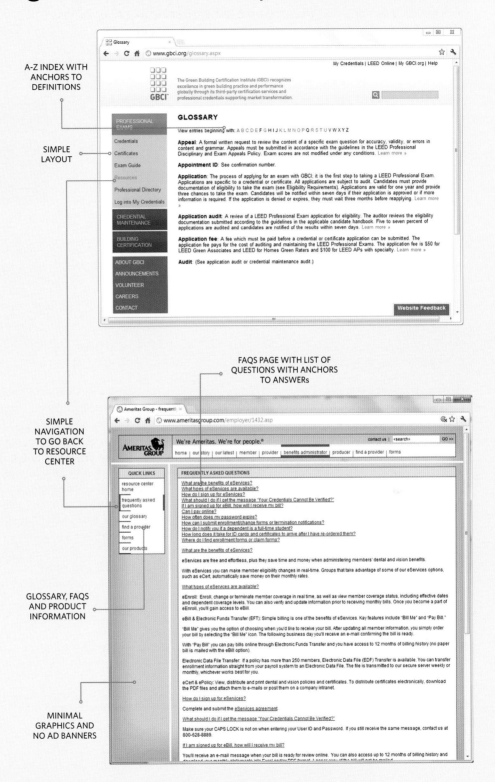

41

Knowledgebase (KB)

A WEBSITE FOR ARTICLES RELATED TO A PARTICULAR KNOWLEDGE DOMAIN

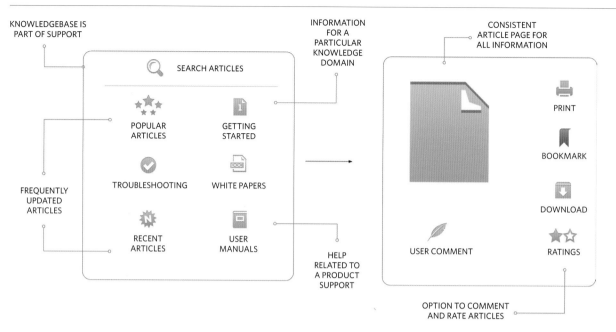

A knowledgebase is an online, automated support system for a particular product. It contains numerous articles, white papers, troubleshooting information, and user manuals and is meant to supplement a product or service by giving information in the form of simple articles. A knowledgebase provides answers to specific product-related questions.

Best Practices and Design Guidelines
- Keep the KB home layout simple with blocks of information
- Avoid heavy graphics, Flash, and banner ads
- Allow advanced search for exhaustive query support
- Have a section for first-time users
- Allow user interaction, comment, and ratings on the article page
- Use icons and styles to add visual cues to different types of information

User Experience
- Have minimal layout to put focus on the content
- Use consistent layout for all article pages
- Use breadcrumb navigation to go back to the KB homepage
- Use light background and follow accessibility guidelines for content

(+) See also **Online Forums** on page 80 and **Resource Center/Help Center** on page 86.

Netop Knowledgebase

The knowledgebase at kb.netop.com is simple and intuitive. use. It categorizes all information into groups and has sections for featured articles and most-recent articles. The theme of the website is very simple with few colors, and it uses Verdana, which is easy to read. The article page has standard options to print, download, bookmark, email, and share.

QUICK ACCESS TO KNOWLEDGEBASE
http://kb.netop.com

CLEAN AND
SIMPLE DESIGN

QUICK AND
ADVANCED
SEARCHES

INFORMATION
CATEGORIES

ARTICLES WITH
NUMBER OF VIEWS
AND UPDATE
INFORMATION

BREADCRUMB
NAVIGATION FOR
QUICK ACCESS TO
CATEGORY AND
TO GO BACK TO
KB HOME

USE OF ICONS
AND SECTION FOR
ATTACHMENTS

Wiki

A WEBSITE THAT CAN BE VIEWED AND MODIFIED BY ANYONE USING THE INTERNET

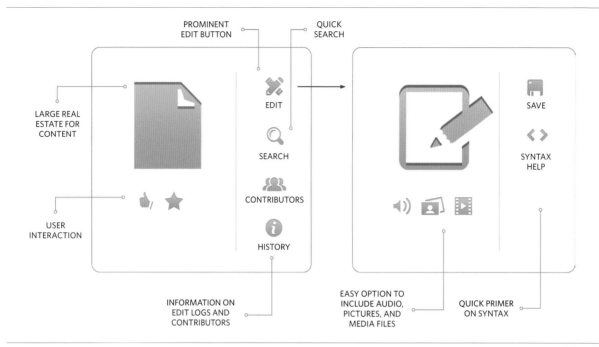

A wiki is a website created for collaboration, where many people come together and pool information. It is a content-management system where anybody can create new pages or edit existing pages of the website. It allows people to work together on the same page and does not require any special knowledge to create or edit pages.

Best Practices and Design Guidelines
- Keep main area of the page for content
- Have simple and consistent structure for all the pages with categories
- Limit use of HTML frames, style sheets, and JavaScript
- Avoid Flash, banner ads, and any other kind of advertisement

User Experience
- Use simple text-based color scheme and easy-to-read fonts
- Avoid any header graphics or graphically rich navigation controls
- Allow editing with plain text as well as rich text with advanced formatting options

(+) See also **Online Forums** on page 80, **Content Management System** on page 112, and **Knowledgebase** on page 88.

Designandmethod.wikispaces.com

The wiki platform, Wikispaces, provides an easy-to-use interface for wiki-based websites. The website has a single page in the beginning that you can start editing for your content. Then, as you link more pages and create them, the website takes shape in an incremental way. The edit page features a rich text box control for easy HTML content creation for the page, and it also allows embedding, files, images, and widgets on the web page.

PROMINENT EDIT BUTTON

USER DISCUSSION COMMENTS AND REVISIONS

MAIN AREA FOR CONTENT

QUICK NAVIGATION WITH HISTORY INFORMATION

QUICK SEARCH

RICH TEXT CONTROL WITH OPTION TO INCLUDE LINK, WIDGET, OR FILE

OPTION TO COMMENT AND DISCUSS PAGE CONTENT

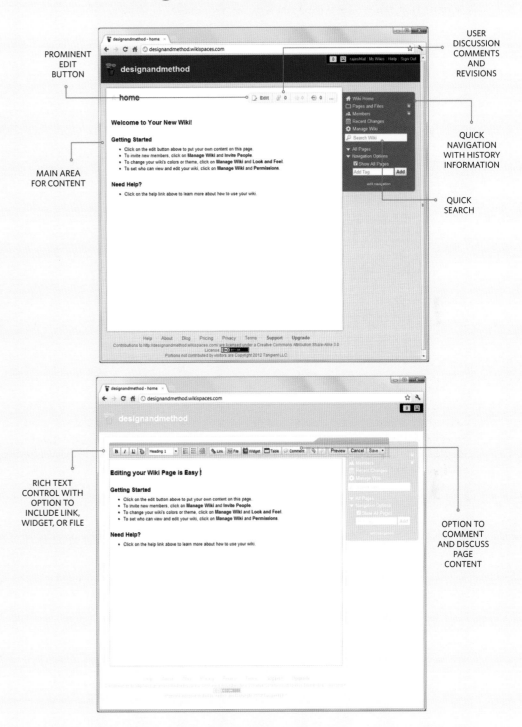

43

Online Surveys

A WEB TOOL FOR COLLECTING INFORMATION FROM WEBSITE VISITORS

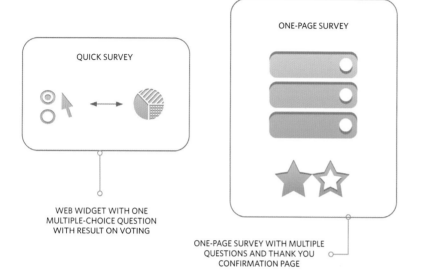

QUICK SURVEY

WEB WIDGET WITH ONE
MULTIPLE-CHOICE QUESTION
WITH RESULT ON VOTING

ONE-PAGE SURVEY

ONE-PAGE SURVEY WITH MULTIPLE
QUESTIONS AND THANK YOU
CONFIRMATION PAGE

MULTIPAGE SURVEY

A WEB WIZARD WITH
PROGRESS BAR FOR A
MULTISTEP QUESTIONNAIRE

An online survey is a web-based tool to collect data from users. It can be in the form of an instant poll, a web widget with a multiple-choice question, or a mini web wizard with multiple pages of questions. It allows online companies to engage users and hear their voices on pressing issues.

Best Practices and Design Guidelines

- For instant poll:
  - Use objective answers with radio buttons or check boxes
  - Show results after taking the poll
  - Randomize answer order to avoid border answer bias (border choice prone to selection)
- Have clear indication ("Finish/End" button) for one-page survey
- Use a multipage survey with progress bar
  - Tell survey completion time in advance
  - Avoid large set of questions in one big table
  - Keep your first survey page simple
  - Keep a fixed set of questions on every page and consistent layout
- Use accessible guidelines for content

User Experience

- Keep questions one line
- Keep subjective questions optional
- Tell user how many more questions are in the survey
- Keep everything on one page

(+) See also **Accessible Web** on page 50 and **Web Widget** on page 98.

TrickofMind.com and Survey Monkey One-Page Example

TrickofMind uses a widget-based survey to engage users. It uses a single question, multiple-choice format, and shows the result. Survey Monkey's one-page survey example uses a pleasing theme and one-page format. The questions have a good amount of white space and the text can be scaled.

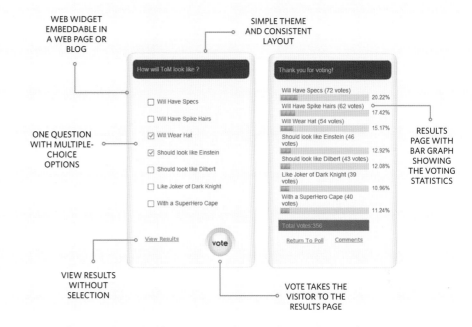

WEB WIDGET EMBEDDABLE IN A WEB PAGE OR BLOG

SIMPLE THEME AND CONSISTENT LAYOUT

ONE QUESTION WITH MULTIPLE-CHOICE OPTIONS

RESULTS PAGE WITH BAR GRAPH SHOWING THE VOTING STATISTICS

VIEW RESULTS WITHOUT SELECTION

VOTE TAKES THE VISITOR TO THE RESULTS PAGE

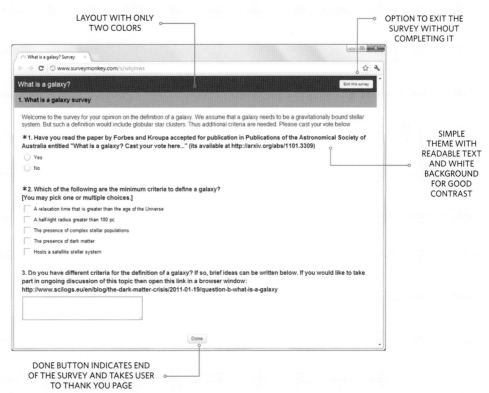

LAYOUT WITH ONLY TWO COLORS

OPTION TO EXIT THE SURVEY WITHOUT COMPLETING IT

SIMPLE THEME WITH READABLE TEXT AND WHITE BACKGROUND FOR GOOD CONTRAST

DONE BUTTON INDICATES END OF THE SURVEY AND TAKES USER TO THANK YOU PAGE

44

Rating App

A UTILITY TO SCORE/VOTE A PRODUCT ONLINE

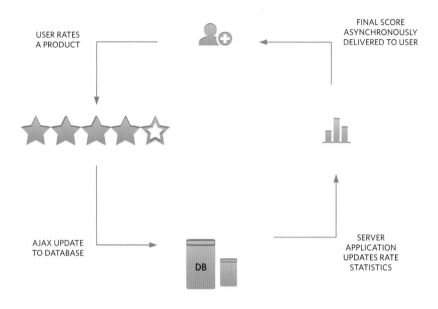

A rating system allows for quality assessment as well as user engagement. It collects feedback from existing customers to improve the product and also provides insightful information to potential customers. Five-star rating systems are quite popular, where the user has an option to give up to a five-star rating, with five being the best score and one, the worst.

Best Practices and Design Guidelines
- Have three distinct states:
  - Current state, with existing scores
  - Active state, when user is selecting a star
  - Rated state, when user has rated the product
- Seamlessly blend rating system with website, occupying least amount of space
- Use Ajax methodology (no page refresh) to add the score in the background
- Design to encourage ratings and be easy to use

User Experience
- Show status while rating and after rating
- Have a rate board with graphics (bar diagrams) for each type of score

(+) See also **Web Widget** on page 98 **Ajax Web Application** on page 114.

AddRating.com and Fendi.com

AddRating.com provides a custom rating widget, which can be embedded in any website. It provides the current score, the active state when the color of the rating "stars" changes to red on mouse hover, and the final state after rating. On the other hand, Fendi.com has a unique built-in, hidden rating system. It shows AM♥R (AM lover) with a number, which shows the number of people that "liked" or clicked AM♥R for that particular item. The rating happens seamlessly in the background and the final number gets updated.

RATING ACTIVE STATE WITH
CURRENT RATING

RATE BOARD SHOWING
STATISTICS FOR EACH TYPE
OF RATING

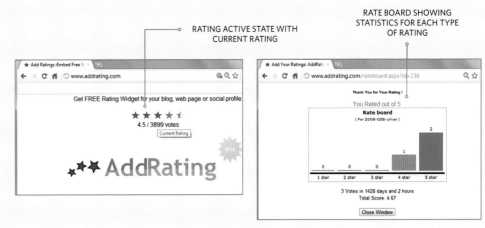

SIMPLIFIED AND UNIQUE RATING
SYSTEM AT FENDI.COM

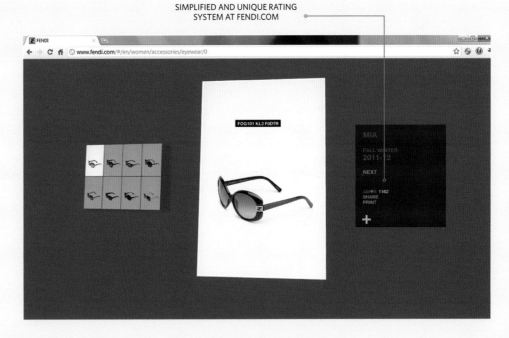

45

Rich Internet Application (RIA)

WEB APPLICATION THAT DELIVERS A RICH, DESKTOP-LIKE EXPERIENCE

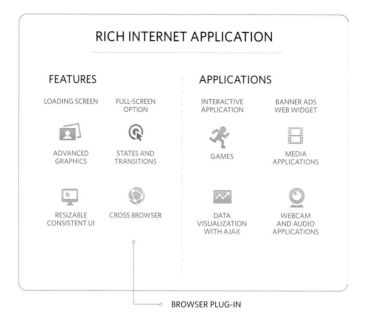

RIA provides interaction and features on a web page with a consistent UI across multiple browsers. RIA is normally used as either an island of rich functionality on a web page or a whole web page. It uses scalable vector graphics, GPU-accelerated animations, 3-D, media, and Ajax. RIAs dominate online gaming, and are used for creating web widgets, banner ads, advanced media players, and Ajax-based sophisticated data visualizations.

Best Practices and Design Guidelines
- Have a progress bar for loading status of RIA
- Ensure RIA has fixed-size application across browsers and platforms
- Use gradients, transparency, and high-quality graphics
- Note that RIA also features a full-screen option

User Experience
- Advanced graphics and seamless animations are expected from RIA
- Use for advanced dynamic and interactive data visualization
- Have a visually rich user interface with state transitions on user activity
- Use up-to-date colors and contrast

(+) See also **Web Widget** on page 98, **Media Player** on page 28, and **Banner Ad** on page 102.

GotMilk.com uses Microsoft Silverlight technology to deliver a full-screen RIA. It uses high-quality graphics. The loading screen sets the stage for a high-quality interactive application, and once loaded, the interactivity with subtle state transitions and clutter-free design delivers an immersive experience.

RICH VECTOR GRAPHICS THAT SCALE WITH BROWSER SIZE WITHOUT LOSING QUALITY

PROGRESS BAR SHOWS LOADING STATUS

RICH TRANSITION AND EFFECTS

PROFESSIONAL RICH GRAPHICS AND ANIMATIONS

INTERACTIVE WITH STATE TRANSITIONS

46

Web Widget

A WEB APPLICATION THAT CAN BE EMBEDDED IN A WEBSITE, BLOG, OR SOCIAL PROFILE

KEY ELEMENTS OF A WEB WIDGET

SINGLE-PURPOSE
MINI UTILITY

CUSTOMIZATION OF
LAYOUT WITH COLOR
PALETTE

SHARING CODE AND
VIRAL DISTRIBUTION

Web widgets are small utilities and add extra functionality to a web page. A web widget can be a visitor count, clock, calendar, or simple feature to subscribe users. Users can go to a widget provider website, customize the widget, and use the generated HTML code to embed it in their website.

Best Practices and Design Guidelines
- Have a visually appealing and easy-to-use widget
- Use four steps for widget customization:
    - Identification to personalize the wizard with user ID
    - Customization of layout, color, and fonts
    - Preview of widget, showing the new custom widget
    - Deployment code to be generated so users can use it on their web page
- Use space effectively without overloading data
- Use little branding and avoid banner ads

User Experience
- Focus widget on one feature
- Make self-explanatory with a default layout and data
- Use default values to get the user started quickly
- Use a seamless, borderless design to fit with any web page
- Avoid asking for login, registration, or emails to use the widget
- Support sharing and bookmarking online through social sharing plug-ins
- Allow custom size with default size to fit on the side navigation

(+) See also **Desktop Widget/Gadget on** page 30.

Flickr Badge allows you to embed your photo gallery in a web page. The customization is a simple step-by-step process that generates HTML code. The HTML code can be embedded in any web page.

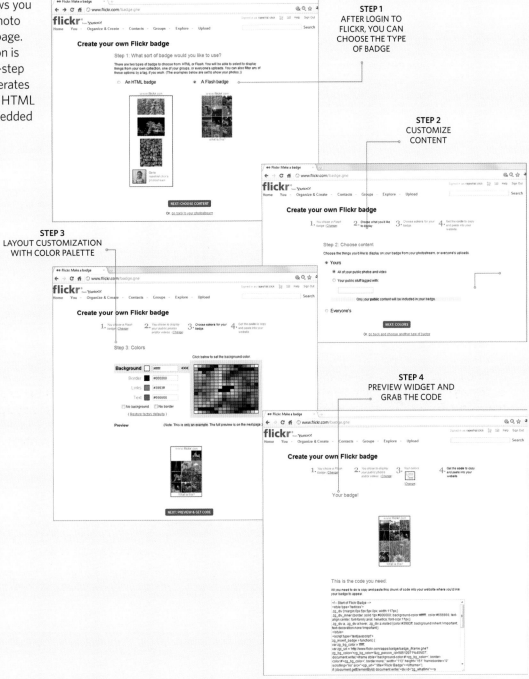

STEP 1
AFTER LOGIN TO FLICKR, YOU CAN CHOOSE THE TYPE OF BADGE

STEP 2
CUSTOMIZE CONTENT

STEP 3
LAYOUT CUSTOMIZATION WITH COLOR PALETTE

STEP 4
PREVIEW WIDGET AND GRAB THE CODE

Book Widget

A BOOK WIDGET ALLOWS YOU TO PREVIEW A BOOK BEFORE YOU BUY IT

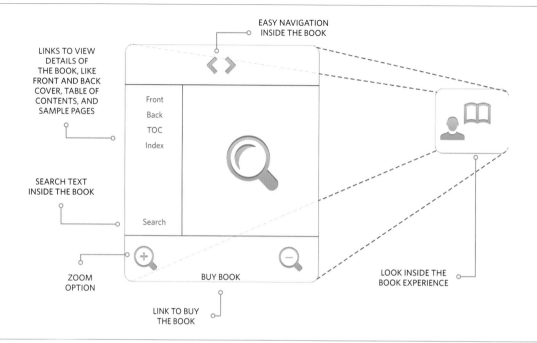

EASY NAVIGATION
INSIDE THE BOOK

LINKS TO VIEW
DETAILS OF
THE BOOK, LIKE
FRONT AND BACK
COVER, TABLE OF
CONTENTS, AND
SAMPLE PAGES

Front

Back

TOC

Index

SEARCH TEXT
INSIDE THE BOOK

Search

ZOOM
OPTION

BUY BOOK

LOOK INSIDE THE
BOOK EXPERIENCE

LINK TO BUY
THE BOOK

A book widget gives online users a look inside the book experience like in a physical bookstore. Users can see the front cover, back cover, table of contents, sample pages, and index, and search inside the book.

Best Practices and Design Guidelines

- Have easy access and navigation to a list of available preview pages
- Allow easy navigation between pages with Previous and Next buttons
- Add full-screen option with ability to zoom in and out
- Allow a search option for keywords in the book
- Have a buy book option

User Experience

- Use page transition animation to give a page-flip experience
- More pages to preview is more useful for the user
- Have quick loading of the pages

⊕ See also **Web Widget** on page 98 and **Desktop Widget/Gadget** on page 30.

Barnes and Noble and Google Book Widget

Barnes and Noble has an easy-to-use interface with navigation and zoom options at the top center. It also shows tiny thumbnails in the bottom to give context to the navigation. The Google book widget has a simpler interface and shows the list of available pages only when you click on the contents link at the top. Both widgets have search options for particular keywords.

EASY NAVIGATION
WITH ZOOM OPTION

BUY
OPTION

LIST OF
AVAILABLE
PAGES FOR
PREVIEW

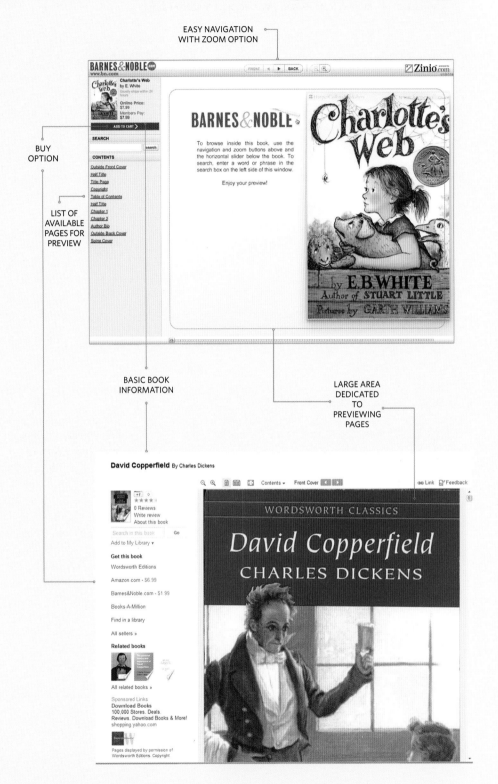

BASIC BOOK
INFORMATION

LARGE AREA
DEDICATED
TO
PREVIEWING
PAGES

48

Banner Ad

A BANNER AD IS A GRAPHICAL WIDGET USED FOR ADVERTISING ON THE WEB

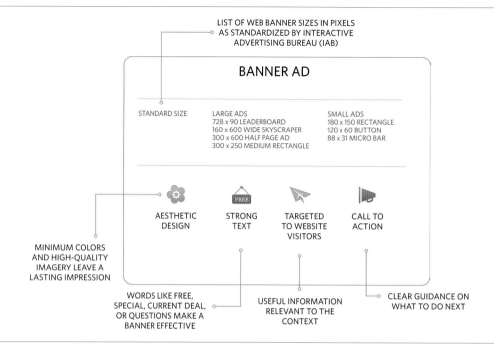

Banner ads are special kinds of web widgets intended to attract traffic to a website. Banner ads normally have a high aspect ratio (wide or tall), containing rich graphics, animations, and sometimes audio, video, and interactive elements. Simple banner ads can be a set of three rotating images.

Best Practices and Design Guidelines

- Make use of rich graphics and dynamic content, like a banner with different local offers
- Have prominent brand incorporation and call to action
- Include a URL in the banner
- Keep rotating banner, three to five frames
- Use no more than 40Kb size for large ads and 10 to 20Kb for smaller ads
- Note the animation recommendation is 15 seconds

User Experience

- Avoid flashy content, bumpy animations, and overly bright colors
- When using media, let the user choose to start and stop audio and video
- Think billboards—don't use more than a few words (seven is optimum)

(+) See also **Rich Internet Application (RIA)** on page 96 and **Web Widget** on page 98.

The design and color choice of the IAB website is professional, grabs users' attention with a question, and has a clear call to action view.

PROFESSIONAL AND SEAMLESS BANNER AD AT INTERACTIVE ADVERTISING BUREAU

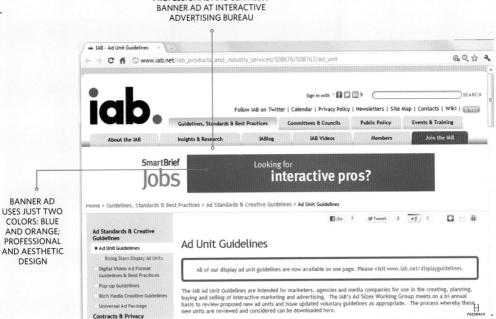

BANNER AD USES JUST TWO COLORS: BLUE AND ORANGE; PROFESSIONAL AND AESTHETIC DESIGN

THREE VIEWS OF SMARTBRIEF JOBS BANNER AD

BANNER STARTS WITH STRONG TEXT, A QUESTION TO ATTRACT ATTENTION

SmartBrief Jobs — Looking for **interactive pros?**

USEFUL INFORMATION EDUCATES USER AND GENERATES INTEREST

CONTEXTUALLY RELEVANT TO IAB WEBSITE VISITOR

SmartBrief Jobs — There are now more than **40,000 IAB SmartBrief subscribers** in your candidate pool.

SmartBrief Jobs — **Click here to post your available jobs.**

SIMPLE CALL TO ACTION

49

Web Slideshow

AN APPLICATION TO SHOWCASE A SERIES OF SELECTED IMAGES OR SLIDES IN A PREDEFINED ORDER

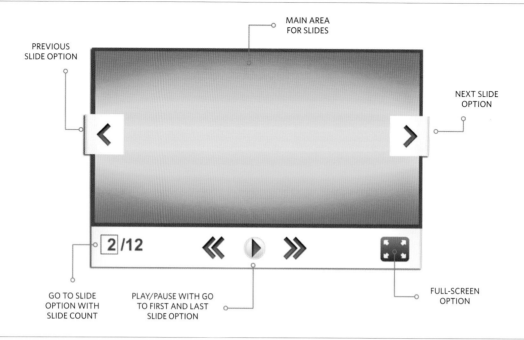

Web-based slideshows are created using rich Internet application technologies like Adobe Flash and Microsoft Silverlight or standard web technologies such as HTML, CSS, and JavaScript. A basic slideshow can be an image rotator with customizable images, whereas an advanced web slideshow might port a desktop presentation like PowerPoint, Keynote, or even PDF into a formatted slide-show application.

Best Practices and Design Guidelines

- Allow viewer control of the slideshow
- Keep the navigation controls outside of the slide content
- Have slideshow controls easily clickable
- Make the transition of the slideshow seamless
- Have thumbnail view of slides for picture/media slideshow

User Experience

- If more than four slides, keep a slide count and go to slide option
- Use translucent, unobtrusive UI controls for the picture slideshow
- Give visual feedback to the current status of loading of next slide
- Support autoplay to next slide with duration of 3 seconds or more

(+) See also **Web Widget** on page 98, **Media Player** on page 28, and **Rich Internet Application (RIA)** on page 96.

Silverlight Slideshow Widget and Flickr Badge

Silverlight Slideshow Widget allows you to include/add a custom set of images, whereas Flickr Badge shows the user photo gallery in full-screen mode.

BASIC SLIDESHOW WIDGET WITH CUSTOMIZABLE DIMENSION AND SLIDES

PREVIOUS, NEXT CONTROLS WITH SLIDE COUNT

FULL-SCREEN OPTION

HTML PHOTO SLIDESHOW AT FLICKR

PROMINENT PREVIOUS AND NEXT BUTTONS

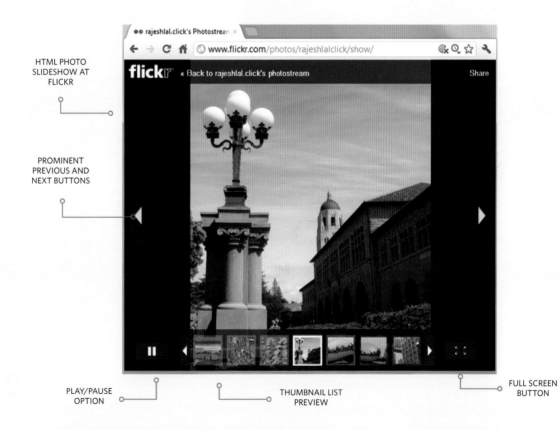

PLAY/PAUSE OPTION

THUMBNAIL LIST PREVIEW

FULL SCREEN BUTTON

50

HTML5 App

AN APP-LIKE EXPERIENCE ON A WEBPAGE USING THE LATEST WEB TECHNOLOGIES

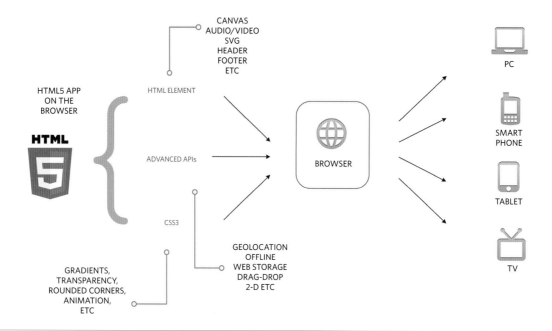

A web app uses advanced HTML5 technologies to create online game, graphics utility, rich Internet application, or media application. HTML5 comes with a new set of HTML elements and advanced web APIs, and supports CSS3, the latest in graphics and animation. It also supports multiple browsers and devices like mobile, tablets, PCs, and TVs.

Best Practices and Design Guidelines
- Have a one-page app
- Understand the design challenges regarding the target device
  - Screen sizes: mobile, 2 to 4 inches; tablet, 7 to 14 inches; desktop, 14 to 27 inches; television, 25 to 65 inches
  - Viewing distance: mobile, 1 foot; tablet, 1 foot; desktop, 2 feet; television, 10 feet
  - Connectivity: Mobile, 3G; tablet, wifi; PC, LAN; TV, LAN
  - Reliability: Mobile, unreliable; tablet, wifi connected; PC, connected; TV, fast connection
  - Input: Mobile, finger; tablet, touch; desktop, keyboard and mouse; TV, D-pad and remote

- Use layout detection and adapt for the device
- Use audio/video elements with a fallback option of Flash

User Experience
- Keep design simple for cross platform
- Use cutting-edge graphics with SVG
- Gracefully degrade for nonsupported browsers
- Use single column to support mobile devices

⊕ See also **Mobile Web App** on page 129 and **Rich Internet Application (RIA)** on page 96.

Online Typography Example at
www.apple.com/html5/showcase/typography

The typography utility shows some of the advanced HTML5 capabilities. It uses HTML elements to render the user interface and CSS3 @font-face to dynamically render custom fonts. Tetrole, an online HTML5 Tetris game at http://ole.im/tetris, also utilizes the HTML5 canvas element to render the Tetris blocks and their animation. It uses CSS3 for color styles and advanced API for local storage to save the score.

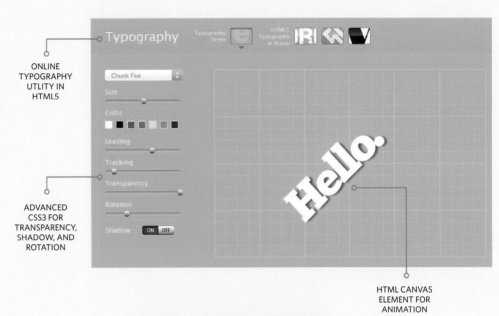

ONLINE TYPOGRAPHY UTLITY IN HTML5

ADVANCED CSS3 FOR TRANSPARENCY, SHADOW, AND ROTATION

HTML CANVAS ELEMENT FOR ANIMATION

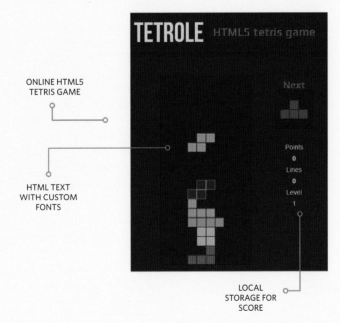

ONLINE HTML5 TETRIS GAME

HTML TEXT WITH CUSTOM FONTS

LOCAL STORAGE FOR SCORE

51

Zooming User Interface (ZUI)

AN INTERFACE THAT USES ZOOM TO INTERACT

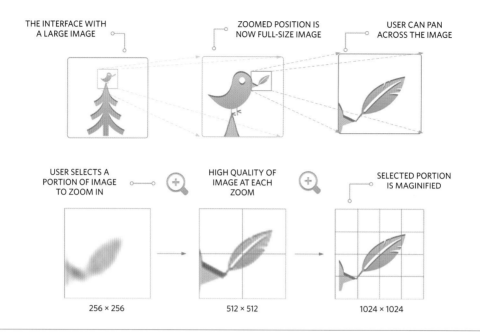

THE INTERFACE WITH
A LARGE IMAGE

ZOOMED POSITION IS
NOW FULL-SIZE IMAGE

USER CAN PAN
ACROSS THE IMAGE

USER SELECTS A
PORTION OF IMAGE
TO ZOOM IN

HIGH QUALITY OF
IMAGE AT EACH
ZOOM

SELECTED PORTION
IS MAGINIFIED

256 × 256

512 × 512

1024 × 1024

A zooming user interface allows a user to zoom in/out of a large interface to see more or less detail. The user can pan across the virtual surface in two dimensions and zoom into elements of interest. As you zoom in, the object becomes more and more clear, first as a small thumbnail, then as you zoom in, it becomes a full-size element and, finally, a high-quality magnified view.

Best Practices and Design Guidelines
- Have a responsive user interface with seamless interaction
- Create a user interface with unobtrusive controls to
  - Zoom in-and-out of the interface
  - Pan across the interface by dragging
  - Have an option for full screen and go back to start screen
- Allow option to zoom in/out using mouse scroll and pan using mouse flick
- Keep an option to set the zoom level

User Experience
- Create smooth transition between the zoom without jerks
- Use translucent buttons
- Start with a default screen zoom level showing the big-picture view

(+) See also **Dashboard/Scorcards** on page 32 and **Rich Internet Application (RIA)** on page 96.

Silverlight uses ZUI to pan across a very large, high-quality image. The example at http://tinyurl.com/DeepZoomSingleImage shows an atlas map that can be zoomed to a particular location.

The example at http://tinyurl.com/DeepZoom-MultipleImage shows a series of images stitched together. Each individual image can be zoomed in for further interaction and information.

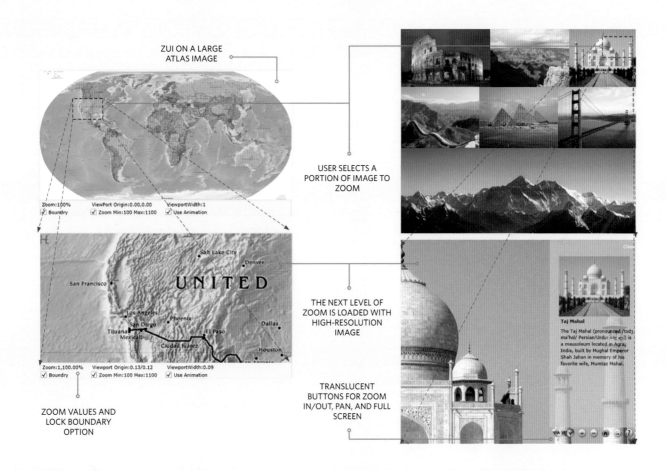

ZUI ON A LARGE ATLAS IMAGE

USER SELECTS A PORTION OF IMAGE TO ZOOM

THE NEXT LEVEL OF ZOOM IS LOADED WITH HIGH-RESOLUTION IMAGE

ZOOM VALUES AND LOCK BOUNDARY OPTION

TRANSLUCENT BUTTONS FOR ZOOM IN/OUT, PAN, AND FULL SCREEN

52

Task Tracking System

AN ONLINE APPLICATION FOR MANAGING A TEAM WORKING ON A PROJECT

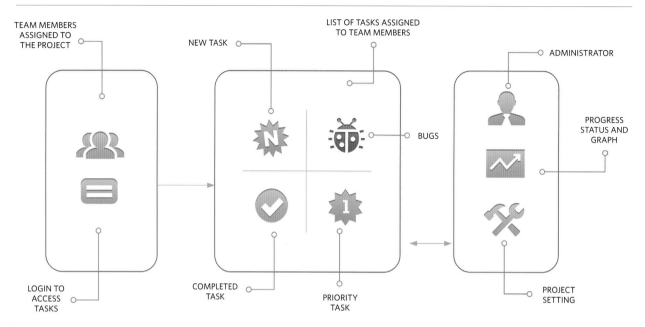

TEAM MEMBERS ASSIGNED TO THE PROJECT

NEW TASK

LIST OF TASKS ASSIGNED TO TEAM MEMBERS

ADMINISTRATOR

BUGS

PROGRESS STATUS AND GRAPH

LOGIN TO ACCESS TASKS

COMPLETED TASK

PRIORITY TASK

PROJECT SETTING

A task tracking system (also called a project management system) is an online system that provides an easy way to monitor a specific task with a team who might be geographically separated. It allows for estimation, planning, organizing, and managing resources related to a particular task.

Best Practices and Design Guidelines
- Have personalized view of the project for each user
- Have a single list with multiple types of issues, bugs, and features assigned to a user
- Show only relevant information to the user and allow filtering and sorting
- Have specific tabs-based interface for project, task list, timetable log, and reports
- Allow login mechanism with different services for members and managers
- Allow filtering and sorting of data

User Experience
- Optimize the display to show maximum information
- Keep the user interface simple and easy to use
- Have a simplistic theme and style with focus on data
- Use standard dashboard with one-page project settings
- Use standard icons for different types of data, such as bugs, features, high priority, and ratings
- Use an easy to understand user interface to encourage collaboration

(+) See also **Online Forums** on page 80 and **Chat Room** on page 35.

Protrackonline.com

This is a project tracking system with web-based login for both team members and administrators. Team members can check multiple types of tasks related to a project, add comments/files to each task, and change the status to complete their own assigned tasks.

ADMINISTRATOR CAN CREATE OR EDIT THE PROJECT

SET TYPES OF STATUS FOR EACH TASK

USER LOGIN TO ACCESS TASKS OR ADMINISTRATOR CAN ACCESS GLOBAL PROJECT SETTINGS

ABILITY TO ADD/REMOVE TEAM MEMBERS

ONGOING LIST OF TASKS FILTERED BY TYPE AND USER

SORT TASK BY USER AND PROJECTS

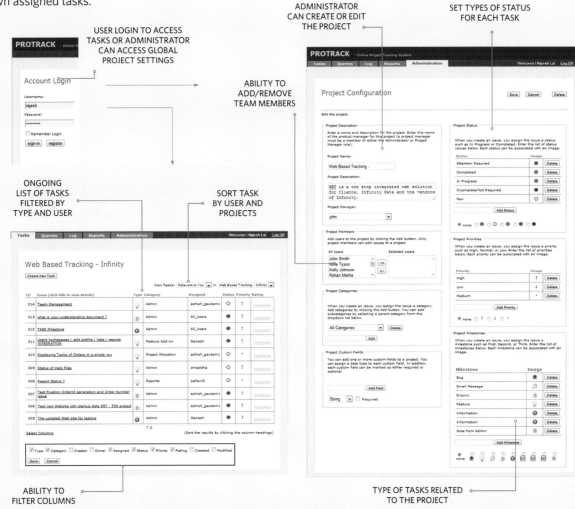

ABILITY TO FILTER COLUMNS

TYPE OF TASKS RELATED TO THE PROJECT

53 Content Management System (CMS)

A WEB-BASED SYSTEM FOR CREATING, EDITING, AND PUBLISHING CONTENT ON A WEBSITE

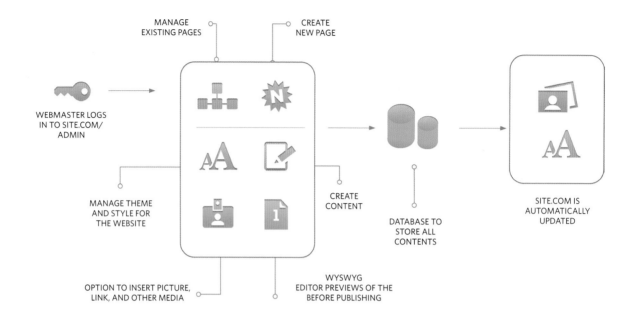

A content management system (CMS) allows a webmaster to manage the content on a website without having to know the technology used to publish the content. It offers a user-friendly way to log in to the admin section and manage content, such as edit text, add images, upload files, insert links, and add new pages.

Best Practices and Design Guidelines

- Have simple web-based access
- Provide flexible editing of content and easy workflow for publishing content
- Have ability to customize theme, background, and style of the website
- Allow changing of style and theme of the website
- Have change preview "what you see is what you get" (WYSWYG) editor to preview changes

User Experience

- Have a dashboard for managing all web pages and content
- Have easy-to-use interface for creating and managing content
- Allow preview of content before publishing
- Allow quick publishing and schedule publishing for a later date

(+) See also **WordPress Theme** on page 64, **Wiki** on page 90, and **Dashboard/Scorecards** on page 32.

Silverlightfun.com Uses a WordPress Content Management System

WordPress provides a quick way of publishing content and makes it easy to manage content. It inherently uses an open-source MySQL database to store and retrieve the content.

DASHBOARD INTERFACE TO MANAGE THE CONTENT

QUICKLY CREATE CONTENT FOR YOUR BLOG

ALLOW CUSTOMIZATION OF THE THEME AND LAYOUT OF THE WEBSITE

HTML OPTION FOR ADVANCED USERS

OPTION TO PUBLISH NOW OR SCHEDULE FOR LATER

OPTION TO INSERT IMAGES AND OTHER FILES

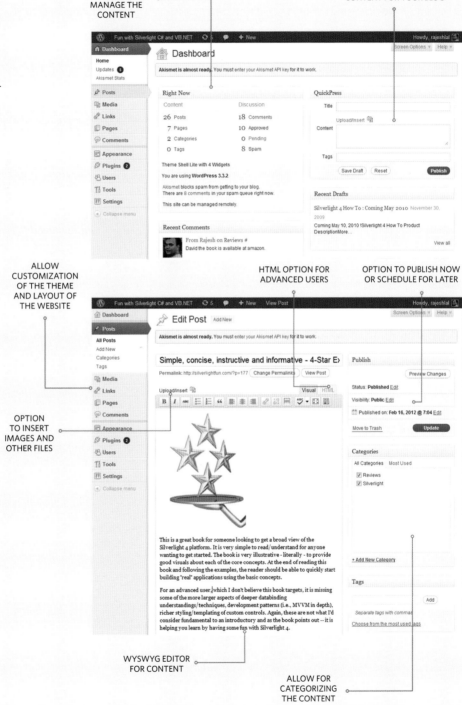

WYSWYG EDITOR FOR CONTENT

ALLOW FOR CATEGORIZING THE CONTENT

54

Ajax Web Application

A RESPONSIVE WEB APPLICATION USING AJAX TECHNOLOGY ON THE CLIENT-SIDE WEB PAGE

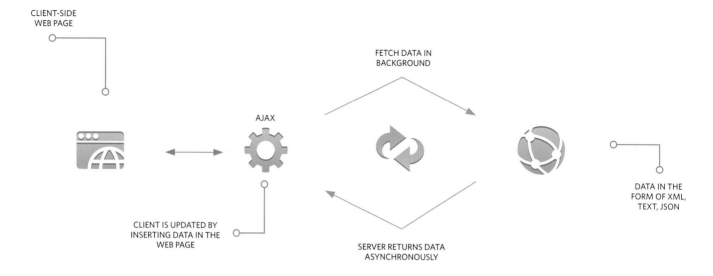

CLIENT-SIDE
WEB PAGE

FETCH DATA IN
BACKGROUND

AJAX

DATA IN THE
FORM OF XML,
TEXT, JSON

CLIENT IS UPDATED BY
INSERTING DATA IN THE
WEB PAGE

SERVER RETURNS DATA
ASYNCHRONOUSLY

The Ajax web application uses AJAX (Asynchronous JavaScript and XML) technique for building websites that are more responsive and have the feel of a desktop application. The application creates a rich client interface that contacts a server in the background to retrieve data and updates the page without reloading the page. The server returns text/XML data that is parsed and rendered back to the web page.

Best Practices and Design Guidelines
- Allow user to trigger Ajax operation
- Have user interface for three steps:
  -UI before the Ajax call
  -Status indicating the call is being made, keeping the UI responsive
  -UI after the data update
- Always tell user when the background process starts
- Use indicators like progress bar and loading animation for background process
- Have alternate method for navigation: Ajax updates are not browser navigable

User Experience
- Desktop-like experience with no page reload
- Clear indications of server call and update are essential

(+) See also **Web Widget** on page 98, **Rating App** on page 94, and **Rich Internet Application (RIA)** on page 96.

Highcharts.com uses Ajax to generate graphs dynamically, using remote data. The data is asynchronously fetched from the server and rendered to create beautiful graphs. LinkedIn uses Ajax to create a user profile widget. On mouse hover, Ajax triggers the background process, during which time the loading animation is shown. The client page is then updated with the user profile.

DATA FROM GOOGLE ANALYTICS ASYNCHRONOUSLY LOADED AND RENDERED

DYNAMICALLY CREATED CONTENT

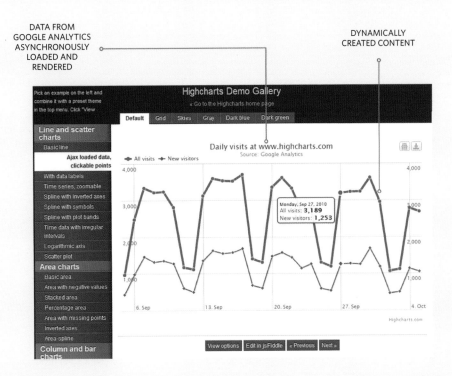

LINKEDIN PROFILE WIDGET USES AJAX

BEFORE AJAX TRIGGER

DURING AJAX CALL, LOADING GIF SHOWS CURRENT STATUS

UI AFTER DATA COMES BACK FROM THE SERVER AND IS RENDERED TO THE PAGE AS A POP-UP

AFTER AJAX CALL RETURNS

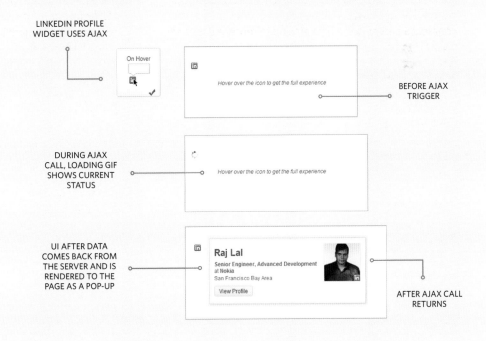

55

Social Design

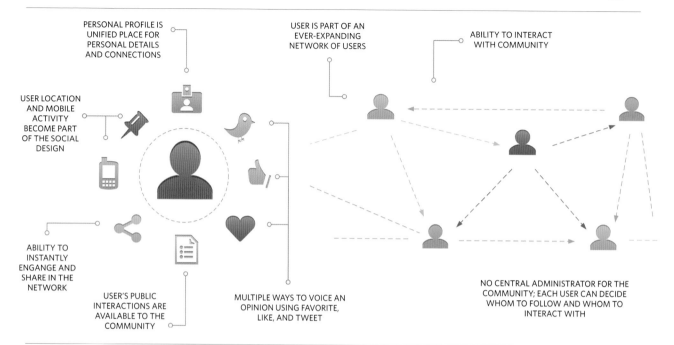

Social design is a way of designing online applications that puts social communication at the center of the interface. It encourages conversation and community development and gives users a sense of belonging to the community. The social design is popular among Web 2.0 websites.

Best Practices and Design Guidelines

- Create a vibrant community around the user interaction
- Allow user to find and connect with existing and new people
- Have customizable and detailed personal profile page
- Show real-time content updates to engage user
- Group users by location and choice, and allow private and public groups within the network

User Experience

- Allow interaction with user's location
- Make the social design easily accessible from mobile phones
- Allow instant sharing of content within the network
- Make it easy to communicate among groups without the need for individual emails

(+) See also **Web 2.0 User Interface Design** on page 120, **User Profile** on page 78, and **Online Forums** on page 80.

Stackoverflow.com

Stackoverflow.com is a collaboratively edited question-and-answer website for programmers. It has a real-time stream of updated interesting content that instantly grabs a programmer's attention.

INTERESTING CONTENT PROMOTED FOR USER ENGAGEMENT

REAL-TIME UPDATED CONTENT

EASY ENGAGEMENT FOR COMMUNITY; NO REGISTRATION FOR VISITORS

OPTION TO INSTANTLY SHARE CONTENT

USER PROFILE PAGE WITH AVATAR, WEBSITE, AND DETAILS

PROFILE PAGE KEEPS A LOG OF USER ACTIVITY

REPUTATION SHOWS USER'S POPULARITY

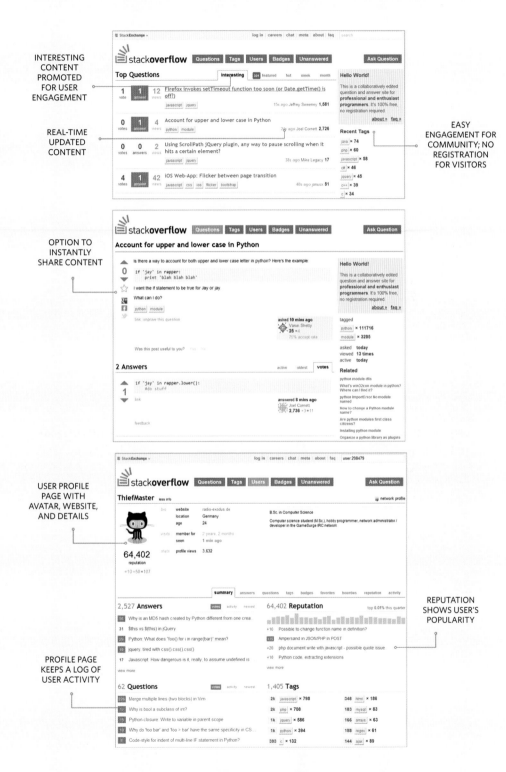

56

Search Engine Optimized (SEO) Web Page

A WEB PAGE INTERFACE DESIGNED FOR HIGHER SEARCH ENGINE RANKING

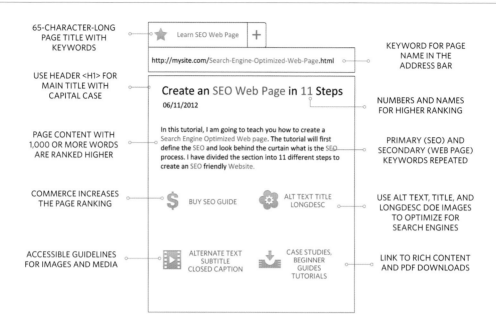

A web page optimized for search engines is crucial if you want to be found by more people on the Internet. Search engine optimization is a series of steps you can take when designing a page that can increase the ranking in the search engine.

Best Practices and Design Guidelines
- Have most important keywords at the beginning of the URL
- Identify primary and secondary keywords for the website and use them in the content
- Use heading tags and capital casing to put emphasis on titles
- Organize the content hierarchically, and use easy-to-read text
- Follow accessible guidelines for text, link, images, and media

User Experience
- Create higher ranking with unique page titles, content, and metadata for each page
- Increase ranking by adding ecommerce
- Include downloads such as case studies and tutorials for better ranking
- Use alternative text for media and descriptive anchors

(+) See also **Homepage** on page 54 and **Single-Page Website** on page 58.

Silverlightfun.com Book Promotion Website

This site follows SEO practices. Name and website meta information contain keywords related to the Silverlight technology.

65-CHARACTER-LONG TITLE

DOMAIN NAME IS SEARCH-ENGINE FRIENDLY

UNIQUE TITLE AND SPECIFIC TOPIC ADD IMPORTANCE IN SEARCH ENGINE RANKING

H1 HEADING TAG USED WITH CAPITALS FOR MOST IMPORTANT TEXT

NEXT IMPORTANT TITLE IN HEADING H2 TAG

MEDIA AND IMAGE WITH PROPER ALT AND TITLE ATTRIBUTE FOR SEO

PDF DOWNLOAD FOR BEGINNER'S GUIDE LINK

BUY OPTION ADDS E-COMMERCE TO THE PAGE, WHICH ADDS RANKING

MORE THAN 1,000 WORDS WITH HIGHLIGHTED KEYWORDS PUT IT IN HIGH RANKING

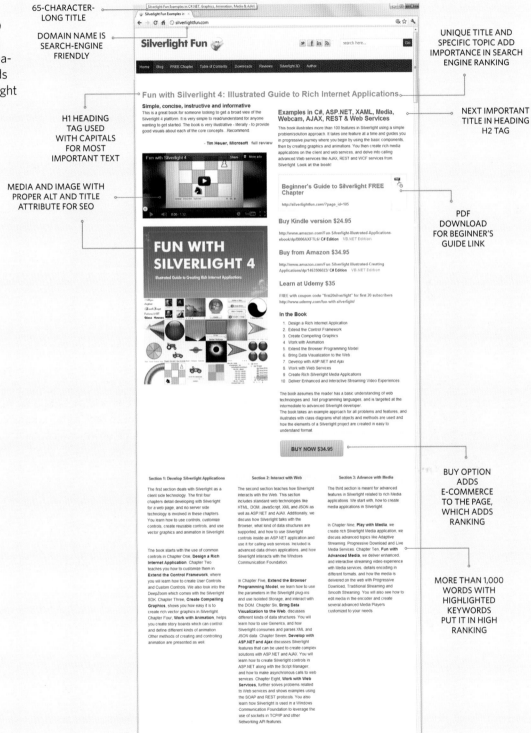

57

Web 2.0 User Interface Design

A VIBRANT STYLE OF WEB ELEMENT DESIGN

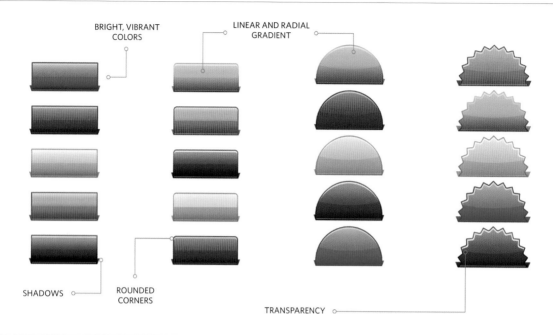

BRIGHT, VIBRANT COLORS

LINEAR AND RADIAL GRADIENT

SHADOWS

ROUNDED CORNERS

TRANSPARENCY

Web 2.0 was coined for the next generation of web-based services, which centered on web-based APIs, collective intelligence, user-generated content, bookmarking, tagging, and more. It was also named after a unique style of web design that became popular with Web 2.0 websites. The predominant websites that defined Web 2.0 style were Flickr, Blogger, Last.fm, StumbleUpon, and Vimeo. These websites feature bright colors, advanced transparent graphics, gradients, glows, and shadows.

Best Practices and Design Guidelines
- Use bright colors and advanced graphic effects, including
    - Transparency
    - Shadows
    - Glows
    - Rounded corners
- Use larger UI elements for better interaction
- Make the UI elements stand out with size bigger than normal
- Use advanced PNG images with transparencies
- Add graphic effects for mouse hover to make the elements interactive

User Experience
- Have graphically rich background wallpapers
- Use vibrant colors
- Make sure the website theme is consistently Web 2.0
- Note that Web 2.0 theme is more popular with community-based websites

(+) See also **Rich Internet Application (RIA)** on page 96, **Homepage** on page 54, and **Social Design** on page 116.

addRating Widget

The addRating widget uses a Web 2.0–style logo with bright colors and shadows. The sample screenshots show the Web 2.0–style web elements, such as the sign-in box, newsletter subscribe box, and weekly poll. The colors stand out and the elements use transparent PNGs and shadow effects.

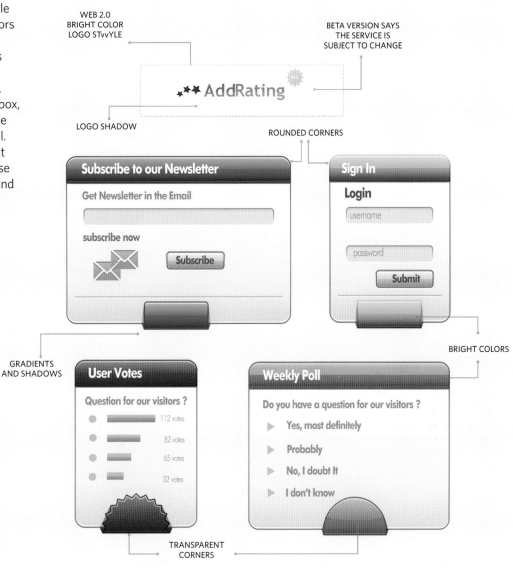

WEB 2.0 BRIGHT COLOR LOGO STvvYLE

BETA VERSION SAYS THE SERVICE IS SUBJECT TO CHANGE

LOGO SHADOW

ROUNDED CORNERS

Subscribe to our Newsletter

Get Newsletter in the Email

subscribe now

Subscribe

Sign In

Login

username

password

Submit

GRADIENTS AND SHADOWS

BRIGHT COLORS

User Votes

Question for our visitors ?

112 votes
82 votes
65 votes
32 votes

Weekly Poll

Do you have a question for our visitors ?

▷ Yes, most definitely

▷ Probably

▷ No, I doubt It

▷ I don't know

TRANSPARENT CORNERS

58

Service-Oriented Architecture (SOA) Design

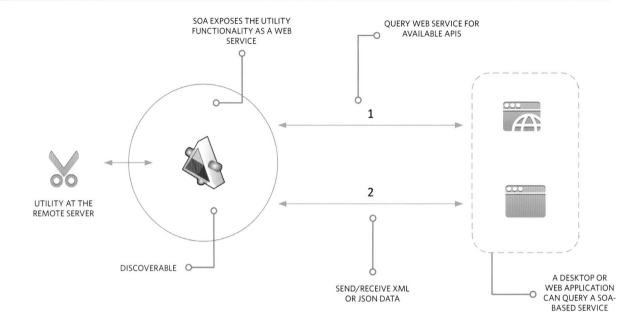

A service-oriented architectural design (SOA) is a web-based utility designed for consumption by other desktop and web applications. It is an online service that can be queried by desktop, web, or mobile application for a particular functionality or regularly updated information, such as weather, stock prices, etc.

Best Practices and Design Guidelines

- Create simple user interface with concise definition of what the service does
- Have neutral theme of the web page where the service is hosted
- Have help page with details on all API exposed by the service
- Have web service page with basic definition and options
- Allow testing on the web with form
- Access service by passing parameters to the URL of the web service
- Show results in the form of XML, JSON, or XHTML

User Experience

- Clear information on the API usage
- Sample test form with data to help user

(+) See also **Website** on page 52 and **Ajax Web Application** on page 114.

Validator.w3.org

W3C Markup Validator is an online service that checks a web page for markup standards. It has a clear definition about the service on the web page and it has a form-based web service, where a user enters the URL and submits it to check the errors on the page. The resulting page is an XHTML file that renders in a browser with result data.

SIMPLE UI WITH NEUTRAL COLOR THEME HAS BECOME A STANDARD FOR WEB SERVICE

CONCISE DEFINITION OF WEB SERVICE

PARAMETER TO SERVICE

ADVANCED OPTIONS

THE WEB SERVICE TAKES PARAMETER DIRECTLY ON THE WEB URL

WEB SERVICE RESULT IN THE FORM OF XHTML

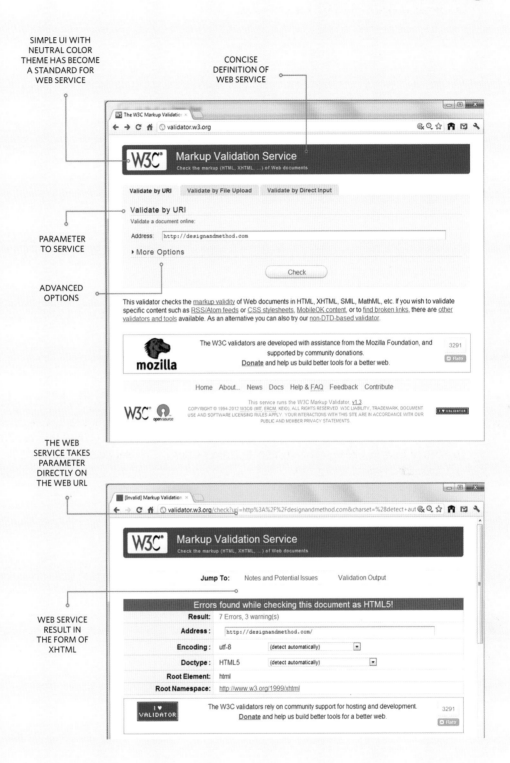

59

Infographics Design

A VISUAL REPRESENTATION OF DATA

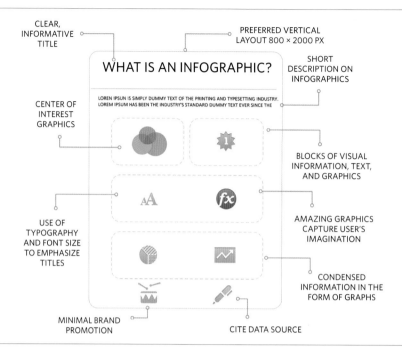

An infographic (information graphic) is a compelling way of showing data with color, type, graphics, illustrations, and charts. It shows complex data in an entertaining and easy-to-understand manner in a one page visual summary. Infographics can be informative, comparative, statistical, and entertaining.

Best Practices and Design Guidelines
- Note most popular sizes of infographics
    - Vertical layout is 800 × 2000+ pixels, easy to embed in blogs
    - Poster size with horizontal layout is 1600 × 1000 pixels
- Make theme based with two or three colors with light gradient
- Use fonts to emphasize important points
- Use sans serif fonts for content text
- Use vector illustrations and icons for each block of information

User Experience
- Try to simplify complex topics
- Keep aesthetic color palette for text and icons
- Make it concise and use clear charts and graphs to show numbers
- Make it visual; avoid being too text heavy

(+) See also **Homepage** on page 54 and **Personal Website** on page 56.

Staying Young Infographics

The infographic features the top ten U.S. cities. It has a clear title and tagline. The main graphic is a U.S. map with pointers to top cities. The information is clearly represented, and there are blocks of information with icons to support the main topic.

TITLE OF THE INFOGRAPHICS

USE OF ARTISTIC FONTS EMPHASIZE TITLE

LIGHT BACKGROUND THEME WITH GRADIENTS

INFOGRAPHICS DESCRIPTION

CENTER OF INTEREST VISUAL DATA

SIMPLE TWO-COLOR THEME KEEPS THE FOCUS ON THE DATA

CONDENSED INFORMATION AND TOP TEN FACTS FROM THE STATISTICS

USE OF SIMPLE ICONS AND IMAGES

CITATION FOR STATISTICAL DATA

— THE BEST & WORST U.S. CITIES FOR —

STAYING YOUNG

Can where you live make you younger or older?

Recent studies suggest that our habits -- good and bad -- can rub off on those around us and influence whether we stay young longer or grow old too fast. See how the habits of citizens in some of the 50 largest U.S. cities stack up in terms of living younger or older.

The Youngest Cities
The Oldest Cities

THE 10 YOUNGEST &

Salt Lake City - Ogden, UT **01**
San Francisco - Oakland - San Jose, CA **02**
Austin - San Marcos, TX **03**
Denver - Boulder - Greeley, CO **04**
Boston - Worcester - Lawrence, MA **05**
Washington - Baltimore, DC-MD **06**
San Diego, CA **07**
Raleigh - Durham - Chapel Hill, NC **08**
Minneapolis - St.Paul, MN **09**
Seattle - Tacoma - Bremerton, WA **10**

THE 10 OLDEST

50 Knoxville, TN
49 Greensboro - Winston-Salem - High Point, NC
48 Nashville, TN
47 Saginaw - Bay City - Midland, MI
46 Cincinnati - Hamilton, OH
45 Tampa - St.Petersburg - Clearwater, FL
44 Oklahoma City, OK
43 Las Vegas, NV
42 Jacksonville, FL
41 Tulsa, OK

What Makes Cities Young or Old

HYPERTENSION
Twin Cities beat the Sooners.
Residents of **Minneapolis** and **St. Paul** have the lowest rates of hypertension in the country. **Tulsa** and **Oklahoma City** rank among the bottom 5 cities for blood pressure.

MARRIAGE
Keep playing those love songs!
Music City, USA, is also Marriage City, USA: **Nashville** ranks #1 in the U.S. for happy marriages. On the other hand, it's the biggest 3 cities, **New York**, **Chicago**, and **Los Angeles**, with the highest rates of being single or unhappily married.

SMOKING
No smoking is the Golden Rule.
4 of the 5 major cities with the fewest smokers are in California: **Los Angeles**, **San Francisco**, **San Diego**, and **Sacramento**. It's the Vols who need to put out the butts: **Knoxville** and **Nashville** are 2 of the cities with the most smokers.

EXERCISE
Go West!
9 of the 10 cities that exercise the most are located in western or mountain states. The 2 least physically active U.S. cities, **Nashville** and **Knoxville**, are both in Tennessee.

SLEEP
NYC isn't really "the city that never sleeps."
Big Apple residents rank #2 in the nation for ZZZs, after #1 **Austin-San Marcos**. Meanwhile, it's the Big A citizens of **Atlanta** who get the least sleep in the country, followed by **Oklahoma City** dwellers.

* Rankings based on responses to questions on the RealAge Test, the online health assessment taken by more than 27 million people since its debut in 1999.

* For the complete ranking of the 50 largest U.S. metropolitan areas, go to RealAge.com.

Adaptive User Interface

AN INTERFACE THAT ADAPTS ITSELF TO A PARTICULAR CONTEXT OR FOR A USER WITH SPECIAL NEEDS

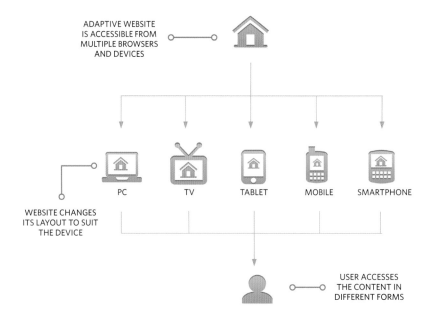

An adaptive user interface changes to suit a particular device, environment, or user. It displays a custom user interface for devices with different sizes and browser capabilities. It resizes the layout, scales the images, and repositions the menus in the website to suit a device.

Best Practices and Design Guidelines

- Use progressive enhancement for developing website around content
- Mobile context, screen size is 2 to 4 inches, distance is 1 foot from the user, in a highly interruptible environment with finger inputs
- Tablet context, screen size is 7 to 14 inches, distance is 1 foot from the user, in casual environment with input touch
- PC context, screen size 14 to 27 inches, distance is 2 feet from the user, on a computer desk, in a focused environment with pixel-accurate input using mouse and keyboard
- TV context, screen size is 25 to 95 inches, distance is 10 feet from the user, used on a comfortable seat/couch, total immersion environment with input using a D-pad or remote

User Experience

- Allow content navigation
  -Accessible navigation sidebar
  -Option to skip to menu
  -Make menu accessible from keyboard
  -Proper nesting of headings
- Follow accessible guidelines for content

(+) See also **Web User Interface (WUI)** on page 48, **10-Foot User Interface** on page 182, and **Accessible Web** on page 50.

Anderssonwise.com uses adaptive web design to customize the website for different device and browser sizes. Based on the context and size, the website displays different images, layout, and image sizes. The layout is fluid and responsive.

ADAPTIVE INTERFACE CHANGES TO ONE COLUMN IN WINDOWS PHONE BROWSER

MOBILE WEBSITE DOES NOT SHOW THE HIGH-QUALITY ARCHITECTURE BACKGROUND IMAGE FOR FAST LOADING

IN A TABLET, THE WEBSITE CHANGES THE LAYOUT TO TWO ROWS

IN A REGULAR COMPUTER BASED ON THE BROWSER WIDTH, THE WEBSITE CHANGES THE LAYOUT TO TWO COLUMNS WITH HIGH-QUALITY IMAGE

IMAGE SIZE ALSO CHANGES WITH THE LAYOUT

Mobile Phone App

A MOBILE APPLICATION THAT USES SPECIFIC DEVICE FEATURES

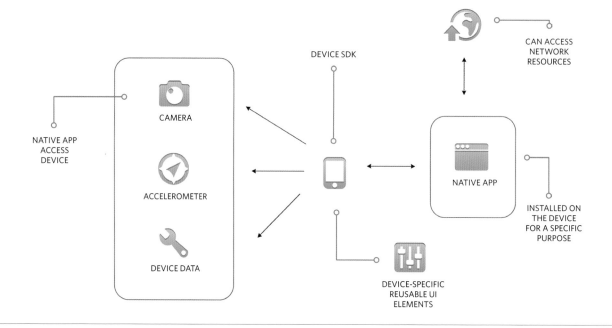

A mobile phone app either arrives preinstalled on the phone (address book, calendar, calculator, maps, and web browser) or can be downloaded from app distribution websites such as app stores. These apps utilize device features such as camera, phone, messaging, and contacts, and uses available device APIs. Native apps give richer immersive experience with offline content and high performance.

Best Practices and Design Guidelines
• Focus on single clear functionality
• Use memorable short titles, professional icon, and precise description
• Utilize target device potential for greater usability
• Create features specific to target users and allow for customization
• Have default settings where possible and store user preferences
• Keep screen layout with plenty of white space and do not clutter
• Use color sparingly and consistently
• Use vibration and other accelerometer features only when they add value

User Experience
• Make it fun and intuitive
• Create custom design
• Ensure app works with interrupted network availability
• Provide clear feedback and allow user to abandon long background processes
• Allow for feedback in the app by including email and online support URL
• Consider making it social by adding ways to share and interact

Mobile Web App

A WEB APP THAT RUNS ON A MOBILE WEB BROWSER

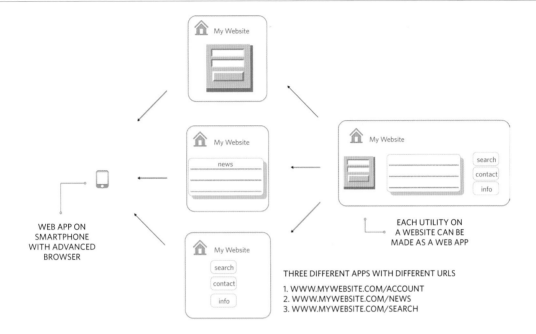

WEB APP ON
SMARTPHONE
WITH ADVANCED
BROWSER

EACH UTILITY ON
A WEBSITE CAN BE
MADE AS A WEB APP

THREE DIFFERENT APPS WITH DIFFERENT URLS

1. WWW.MYWEBSITE.COM/ACCOUNT
2. WWW.MYWEBSITE.COM/NEWS
3. WWW.MYWEBSITE.COM/SEARCH

Mobile web app (MWA) is an HTML5-based app targeted to smartphones with advanced browsers. MWAs use HTML5 and CSS3 technologies that allow for advanced APIs, styles, and animations that make the web app look, behave, and function as a native app. MWAs are meant for single purpose and quick utility. The functionality can be mortgage calculator, current gold price, or quick medical aid.

Best Practices and Design Guidelines

- Keep one idea in one screen, and don't overload data
- Keep the input to a minimum
- Use 100 percent width to accommodate multiple size in multiple mobile devices
- Optimize the display for vertical scrolling
- Use big, touch-friendly buttons
- Have UI for both landscape and portrait

User Experience

- User expects fast load time, so optimize launch screen and keep all file sizes small
- If login is required, use automatic login after first time
- Inform user when loading data from network
- Use image sprites, in page CSS, and JavaScript for minimum number of server trips
- Consider offline user experience with limited functionality with local storage
- Use advanced CSS3 style, transparency, transitions, and animations for great experience

See also **Mobile Website** on page 131, **Mobile Phone App** on page 128, and **HTML5 App** on page 106.

Hybrid App

A MOBILE APP THAT USES EMBEDDED BROWSER TECHNOLOGY TO ACCESS WEB CONTENT

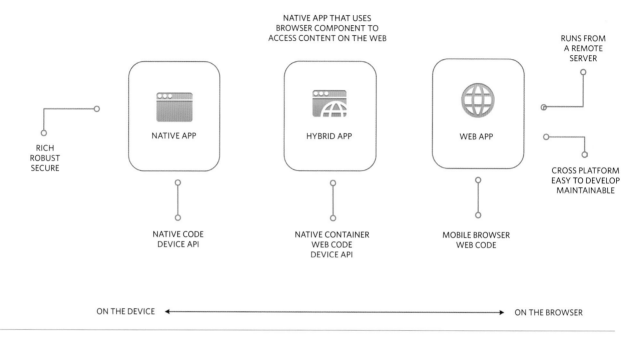

A hybrid app is a web app packaged as a mobile app. It uses an embedded browser to access content from the web. It is ideal for apps with content on the web but needs device access like GPS, local cache, etc. Examples are specialized medical apps and map applications.

Best Practices and Design Guidelines
- Make hybrid apps straightforward
- Mimic the UI of the native app
- Use each screen for a single purpose
- If used for lot of content, use categorization with a maximum of eight categories
- Consider offline mode in hybrid with local caching
- Use hybrid app for monetizing opportunities, branding, and advertising

User Experience
- Use local assets for main categorization and dynamic content from the network
- Inform user when accessing network and location resource
- Cache user's most recent items for offline/low connectivity situation
- Have login for premium content

(+) See also **Mobile Website** on page 131, **Mobile Web App** on page 129, and **Desktop Widget/Gadget** on page 30.

Mobile Website

A SCALED-DOWN VERSION OF AN ONLINE WEBSITE TO PROVIDE A BETTER EXPERIENCE ON MOBILE DEVICES

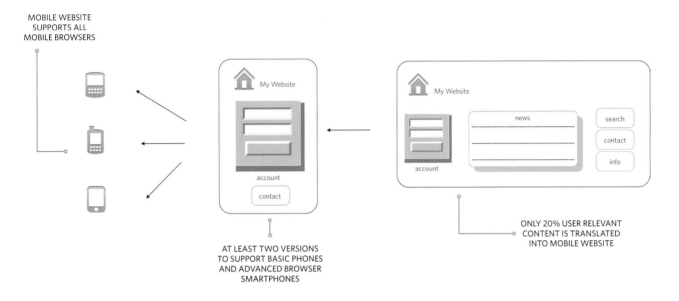

MOBILE WEBSITE
SUPPORTS ALL
MOBILE BROWSERS

AT LEAST TWO VERSIONS
TO SUPPORT BASIC PHONES
AND ADVANCED BROWSER
SMARTPHONES

ONLY 20% USER RELEVANT
CONTENT IS TRANSLATED
INTO MOBILE WEBSITE

A mobile website provides key functionalities of a website in a mobile device. It is designed to work on smartphones as well as most of the standard mobile phones. A mobile website may have multiple UIs for standard phones and smartphones. It displays UI and functionality based on the feature available on the phone browser.

Best Practices and Design Guidelines
- Select top 20 percent functionality of the website
- Use simple navigation and limit to three levels
- Use single-column layout, with three rows
     -Top for notification
     -Middle for content
     -Bottom for input
- Allow website to scale for all mobile browser layouts for both portrait and landscape
- Allow information to flow downward and make it scroll vertically
- Optimize blocks of information
- Do not use pop-ups, mouse hover, or auto refresh
- Avoid external links, frames, and Ajax
- Keep a link to regular website

User Experience
- Use simple words for links and buttons
- Have brief, focused interaction, with minimum input
- Use big, touch-friendly links and buttons
- Make accessible from phone keys/smart keys
- Limit advertising
- Consider a text-only version for mobile phones with limited browsers

See also **Mobile Website App** on page 129, **Mobile Phone App** on page 128, and **Desktop Widget/Gadget** on page 30.

Information App

A MOBILE APPLICATION THAT DISPLAYS FREQUENTLY UPDATED DATA FROM AN ONLINE SERVICE

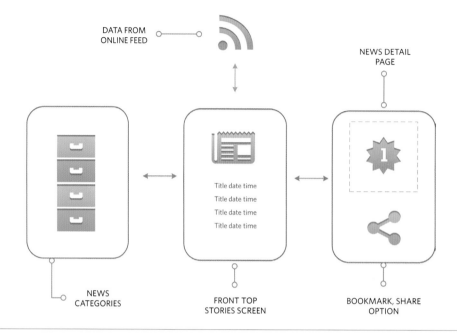

An information app displays an at-a-glance view of current news from a frequently updated online source. The data source can be an online RSS feed or a remote XML/REST-based web service. The information can come from a blog, a news website, or even a social network update. Some examples are stock tickers, RSS feed readers, currency converters, or real-time traffic data.

Best Practices and Design Guidelines

- Have home screen frequently updated with latest news and top entries
- Have easy-to-use, at-a-glance view of information for the home screen
- Keep design content focused
- Keep the top story above the scrollbar
- Leverage images/thumbnails whenever possible
- Have simple navigation between the list screen and the detail screen to display full news
- Have option to share the information by email, social networks, etc

User Experience

- Avoid splash screens
- Do not mix content types—keep one task in one screen
- Have indicator for data loading; no Internet or other warnings
- Have minimal advertisements
- Have an option to bookmark

(+) See also **Mobile Ads** on page 158 and **Mobile Web App** on page 129.

Associated Press News App for Nokia N9

The Associated Press News App for Nokia N9 has a simple and effective user interface. The default screen is the category screen with multiple topics to choose from. Once the user chooses a topic, he lands on a top stories page with thumbnail images.

SMALL LOGO FOR BRANDING

IMAGE THUMBNAILS AND NO DIVIDER LINES BETWEEN HEADLINES

TOP HEADLINES FOR A PARTICULAR CATEGORY

CATEGORY PAGE FOR DIFFERENT TOPICS

EASY, SEAMLESS NAVIGATION

ADVERTISEMENT

HALF-SCREEN QUAILITY IMAGE DISPLAY

FULL NEWS WITH DATE, TIME, AND RATINGS

OPTION TO SHARE THE NEWS AND SAVE

66

Mobile Utility App

A MOBILE APP FOR SIMPLE DEVICE-RELATED TASKS

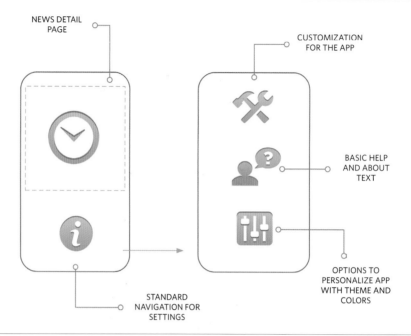

NEWS DETAIL
PAGE

CUSTOMIZATION
FOR THE APP

BASIC HELP
AND ABOUT
TEXT

OPTIONS TO
PERSONALIZE APP
WITH THEME AND
COLORS

STANDARD
NAVIGATION FOR
SETTINGS

A utility app is an app designed to enable fast access to frequently used features, such as the battery, clock, calculator, etc. It uses device API (Application Programming Interface, which functions to access information and features of the device) to get access to advanced features of the mobile operating system and hardware.

Best Practices and Design Guidelines
- Keep the app simple and focused on a single task
- Allow for customization and personalization
- Make interface intuitive with no help required
- Do not use splash screens or banner ads
- Allow the app to work offline

User Experience
- Make it quick and easy to use
- Provide fast loading with no banner ads
- Utilize device capabilities and API
- Set default values; don't ask user to set up the first time
- Avoid login and sign up

(+) See also **Mobile Phone App** on page 128.

Windows Phone Night Stand Alarm Clock and iPhone QlockTwo

The Windows phone night stand clock gives a modern alarm look to the app. Users can create and customize alarms and personalize the color display. On the other hand, the iPhone's QlockTwo app shows time in simple words. It's intuitive to use but also has an information screen for language customization and basic help. The QlockTwo app also features an About screen (not shown), with information about the company and contact details.

ONE-SCREEN APP FOR SHOWING TIME

SETTINGS TO CHANGE LANGUAGE AND BASIC HELP

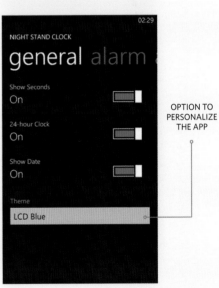

OPTION TO PERSONALIZE THE APP

STANDARD ICON FOR SETTINGS INFORMATION

67

Lifestyle App

A MOBILE APP THAT HELPS US WITH EVERYDAY LIFE

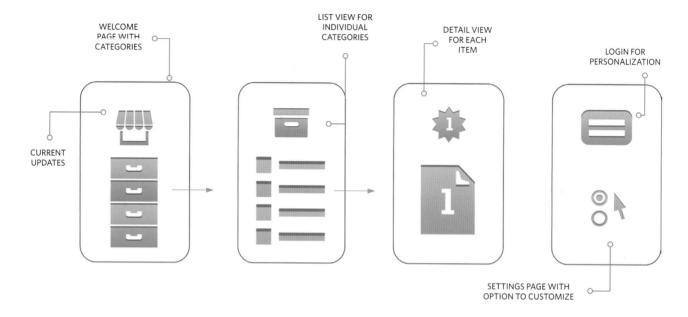

WELCOME PAGE WITH CATEGORIES

LIST VIEW FOR INDIVIDUAL CATEGORIES

DETAIL VIEW FOR EACH ITEM

LOGIN FOR PERSONALIZATION

CURRENT UPDATES

SETTINGS PAGE WITH OPTION TO CUSTOMIZE

A lifestyle app is a simple app for everyday use. It can be related to shopping, fashion, real estate, cooking, culture, travel, sports, and more. The app enriches our daily life by providing simple and useful information at the tip of our fingers. Lifestyle apps feature dynamic and regularly updated information that keeps them interesting and relevant.

Best Practices and Design Guidelines

- Have "today" screen for current information
- Have settings screen with optional login for personalization
- Categorize information into list view and detail view
- Keep the landing screen fresh and updated with relevant and interesting information
- Use standard mobile list view user interface for each category
- Allow interacting with the information on the detail page
- Use optional login in the setting screen for personalization of information

User Experience

- Have straightforward utility with up-to-date information
- Keep the data current
- Allow access to device data such as GPS, maps, gallery, and camera
- Save user preferences for personalized information
- Don't mandate user login to access information
- Make it social by integrating sharing options

(+) See also **Information App** on page 132 and **Branded App** on page 148.

The Trulia app helps users search for homes. It uses a straightforward approach with a home screen that contains individual categories for the search. Once the user selects, say, Open House, it shows a list of open houses in the area. It uses the built-in GPS and also has integrated maps for a big-picture view of the area. It also allows you to save your favorites by logging in to your account.

STRAIGHTFORWARD HOME SCREEN WITH CATEGORIES

OPTIONAL LOGIN TO SAVE FAVORITES

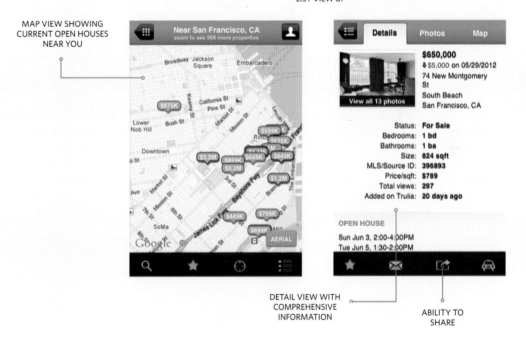

LIST OF CURRENT OPEN HOUSES IN LIST VIEW UI

MAP VIEW SHOWING CURRENT OPEN HOUSES NEAR YOU

DETAIL VIEW WITH COMPREHENSIVE INFORMATION

ABILITY TO SHARE

68 Address Book

A MOBILE APP TO MANAGE YOUR CONTACTS' ADDRESSES

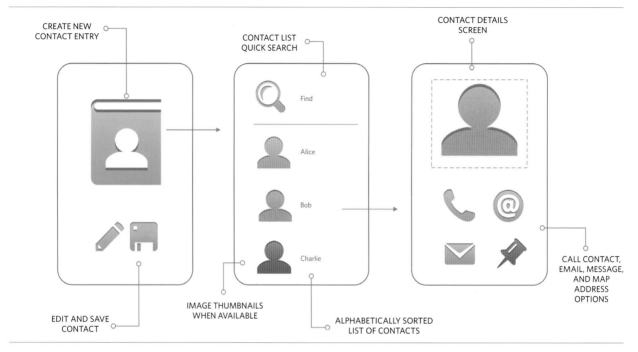

CREATE NEW
CONTACT ENTRY

CONTACT LIST
QUICK SEARCH

CONTACT DETAILS
SCREEN

Find

Alice

Bob

Charlie

CALL CONTACT,
EMAIL, MESSAGE,
AND MAP
ADDRESS
OPTIONS

EDIT AND SAVE
CONTACT

IMAGE THUMBNAILS
WHEN AVAILABLE

ALPHABETICALLY SORTED
LIST OF CONTACTS

An address book stores a list of contacts sorted by name in alphabetical order. It gives users a utility to quickly find a contact and call, instant message, or email. It typically contains the contact's full name, picture, email address, work and home addresses, personal website URL, phone numbers, and personal notes about that contact.

Best Practices and Design Guidelines

- Allow adding contact with minimal required information
- Have sorted contact list page with photo thumbnails
- Have add new contact, edit, and delete options
- Allow quick access to contacts in address book
- Provide option to search for contacts by name
- Provide detail page with option to call, email, or message contact

User Experience

- Have easy setup and quick access
- Allow advanced alphabet selection in contact list page for quicker access
- Have name visible with readable font size and good contrast with the background
- Allow import and export of contact list from a standard address book format
- Allow social integration of contacts

(+) See also **Mobile Phone App** on page 128 and **Web Widget** on page 98.

People Application in Windows Phone Lumia

The address book in Windows Phone Lumia is alphabetically sorted with the option to search for contacts and quickly add a new contact. It has a unique feature that lets you go to a particular letter in the alphabet in the list.

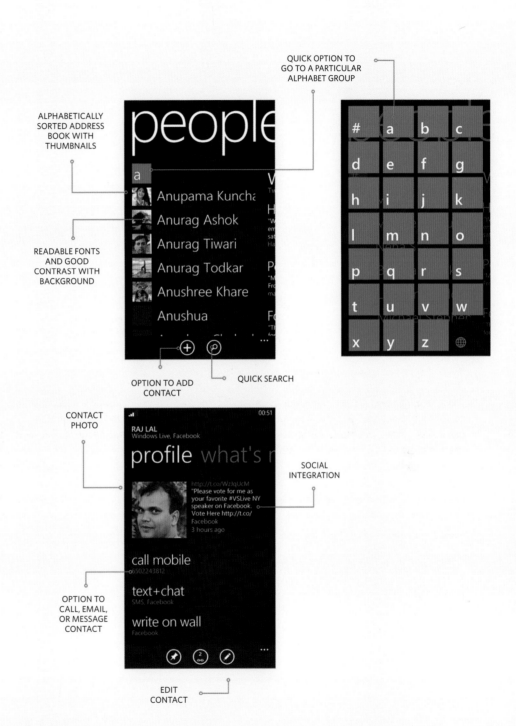

ALPHABETICALLY SORTED ADDRESS BOOK WITH THUMBNAILS

QUICK OPTION TO GO TO A PARTICULAR ALPHABET GROUP

READABLE FONTS AND GOOD CONTRAST WITH BACKGROUND

OPTION TO ADD CONTACT

QUICK SEARCH

CONTACT PHOTO

SOCIAL INTEGRATION

OPTION TO CALL, EMAIL, OR MESSAGE CONTACT

EDIT CONTACT

Camera App

A MOBILE APP FOR USING THE CAMERA

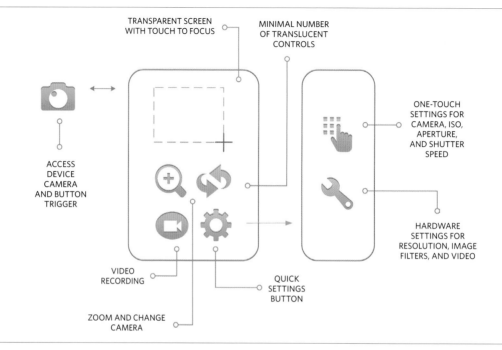

TRANSPARENT SCREEN WITH TOUCH TO FOCUS

MINIMAL NUMBER OF TRANSLUCENT CONTROLS

ACCESS DEVICE CAMERA AND BUTTON TRIGGER

ONE-TOUCH SETTINGS FOR CAMERA, ISO, APERTURE, AND SHUTTER SPEED

HARDWARE SETTINGS FOR RESOLUTION, IMAGE FILTERS, AND VIDEO

VIDEO RECORDING

QUICK SETTINGS BUTTON

ZOOM AND CHANGE CAMERA

A camera app provides easy access to a mobile phone's camera. The camera app is made as an overlay on the camera view window with translucent controls providing full-screen display for camera view. A camera app is an integrated native app and can have advanced features such as access to contacts, GPS information, photo gallery, and picture sharing.

Best Practices and Design Guidelines
- Allow users to go straight to the camera view
- Use transparent controls with outlines
- Allow quick zoom and switch to video mode option
- Keep all the settings touch/tap friendly
- Have a minimum number of camera settings
- Have settings page with one-touch settings for photo and video

User Experience
- Make it quick to use and easy to share
- Provide fast loading time and quick saving while taking photographs
- Have automatic power-save mode when not using the camera after 1 minute
- Have one-touch camera settings with option to default all
- Provide easy geotagging and sharing of photographs

(+) See also **Mobile Phone App** on page 128, **Photo App** on page 142, and **Near Field Communication (NFC) App** on page 156.

NOKIA N9 Camera App

The N9 camera app has a single full-screen transparent view for lens display with translucent controls. It has a quick shortcut for flash and allows switching from camera to video mode. The app features power-save mode and one-touch settings for all camera options. It also gives you easy access to the photo gallery, which lets you share photos through the Internet, Bluetooth, or NFC.

TRANSPARENT SCREEN FOR LENS VIEW DISPLAY

TRANSLUCENT CONTROLS

ONE-TOUCH CAMERA SETTINGS

TAP TO FOCUS

SWITCH TO CAMERA/ VIDEO

ACCESS TO PHOTO GALLERY

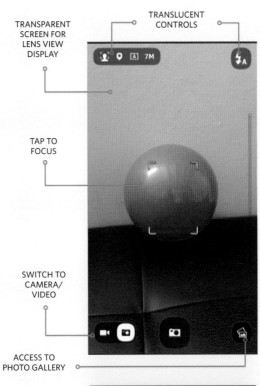

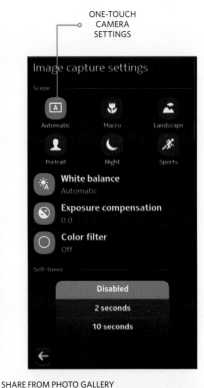

SHARE FROM PHOTO GALLERY

POWER SAVE MODE

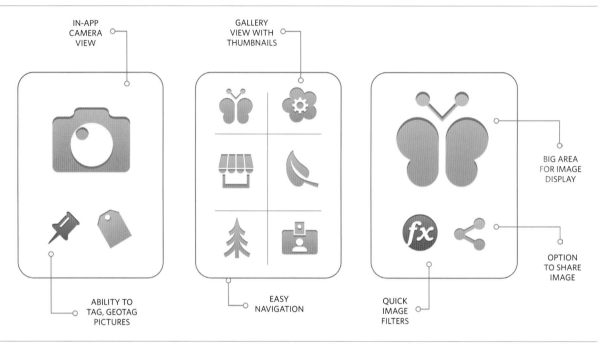

A photo app uses a camera application to instantly take pictures, tag them, and share them with social networks. The application features basic image filters, such as edit and crop photos, before sharing. It uses the phone's camera to take pictures and a gallery to save them.

Best Practices and Design Guidelines
- Allow access to device gallery for picture storage
- Access device contacts for photo sharing
- Have gallery screen for browsing multiple pictures
- Integrate with camera application
- Have screen for image enhancement
- Provide easy navigation and quick filters for image enhancements
- Ask for geotagging and allow users tags in the photograph

User Experience
- Have quick photo-taking capabilities, easy sharing, and fun
- Have an in-app camera experience
- Give camera UI-transparent elements
- Show previews for image filters and allow undo
- Keep navigation easy
- Make it fun with custom picture effects

+ See also **Camera App** on page 140 and **Web Widget** on page 98.

iPhone Instagram App

This app is completely integrated with the iPhone; it uses an in-app camera and saves the photos in the picture gallery. The gallery is available inside the app, which can be then enhanced with custom effects. The app also allows social network integration and even uses contact data to share photos. Overall, the user experience is very seamless and effective.

PHOTO APP GALLERY VIEW OPTIMIZED FOR DISPLAY

THUMBNAILS WITHOUT TITLES

SIMPLE NAVIGATION FOR QUICK PHOTO SHARING

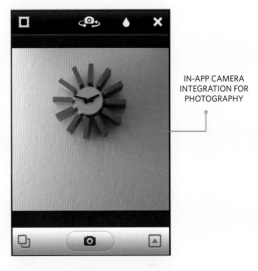

IN-APP CAMERA INTEGRATION FOR PHOTOGRAPHY

SCREEN VIEW OPTIMIZED FOR DISPLAY

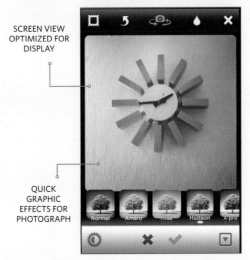

QUICK GRAPHIC EFFECTS FOR PHOTOGRAPH

SOCIAL NETWORK INTEGRATION FOR INSTANT PHOTO SHARING

71

Mobile Game App

AN ELECTRONIC GAME APPLICATION FOR MOBILE DEVICES

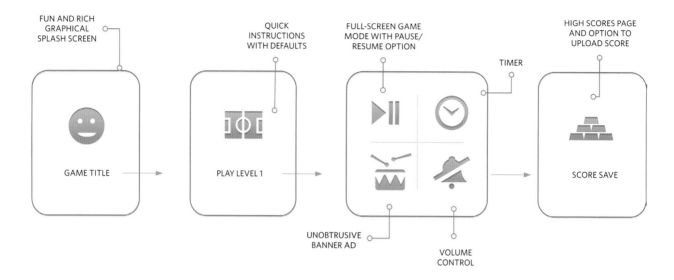

FUN AND RICH
GRAPHICAL
SPLASH SCREEN

GAME TITLE

QUICK
INSTRUCTIONS
WITH DEFAULTS

PLAY LEVEL 1

FULL-SCREEN GAME
MODE WITH PAUSE/
RESUME OPTION

TIMER

UNOBTRUSIVE
BANNER AD

VOLUME
CONTROL

HIGH SCORES PAGE
AND OPTION TO
UPLOAD SCORE

SCORE SAVE

A mobile game app is a video game played on mobile devices. It provides quick entertainment on the go. Current smartphone technology allows innovative games with dazzling graphics and animation. It utilizes device sensors such as accelerometers, gyrometer, camera APIs, and geolocation information to give a much more immersive experience.

Best Practices and Design Guidelines
- Have option for quick play/pause
- Have full-screen game mode with no obtrusive UI controls
- Use transparent buttons for Pause and Volume Control
- Utilize device hardware capabilities and APIs for a richer experience
  - Multiplayer games using device's wireless and Bluetooth
  - Location-based games using GPS information
  - Integrated camera and contacts

User Experience
- Have the game load quickly
- Allow quick access to pause and save game
- Have auto save and sleep mode
- Do auto pause when a notification shows up
- Save user preferences and settings information for next game

(+) See also **Games UI** on page 184, **Natural User Interface** on page 194, and **Mobile Ads** on page 154.

Optime Software's Free Tic Tac Toe Game

Tic Tac Toe is a great example of a popular mobile game. Because the mobile user is in a distractive and dynamic environment, and the engagement level is much lower than with a PC game, having quick start and play is important. The game features a quick splash screen with a start screen containing default settings. Users can select a game level and name, and start to play.

SPLASH SCREEN FOR GAME COMPANY

SIMPLE START PAGE

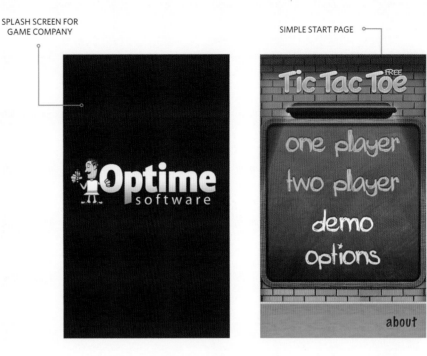

RICH GRAPHICS AND ANIMATIONS

FULL-SCREEN GAME MODE

SETTINGS TO START THE GAME WITH DEFAULTS

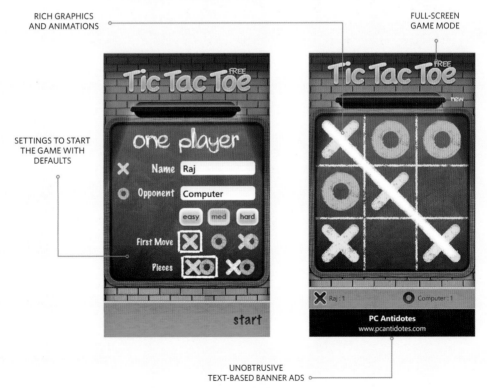

UNOBTRUSIVE TEXT-BASED BANNER ADS

72

Location Aware App

AN APP THAT UTILIZES DEVICE LOCATION TO PROVIDE LOCAL INFORMATION

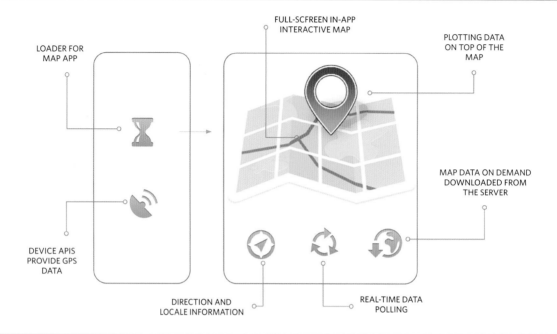

Location-aware apps use a mobile phone's built-in GPS and Internet services to find the device's current location. Based on the location, the app is able to show nearby points of interest, calculate the route to an address, and even locate close friends and family. These apps use the locale information from the calculated geocoordinates to present interesting information to the user.

Best Practices and Design Guidelines
- Have a map screen showing device's current location
- Have a way to interact with the points of interest
- Have loading screen for latency for map initializing and retrieving GPS
- Ask for permission from the user to access device's GPS data
- Have interactive in-app map application with zoom/drag and drop

User Experience
- Keep the app useful with interesting information
- Keep an option to go back to current device location on the map
- Allow adding user's custom data on the map
- Provide feedback with busy, warning, and error indicators
- Update status when fetching real-time data from the Internet
- Tell user what data is being used and shared

(+) See also **Mashup App** on page 178 and **Web Widget** on page 98.

This app is a location-based service using a mobile device's location and a map to show the location of family members. The service requires a monthly subscription from AT&T. Information provided is real time and is updated every few minutes.

LOCATION-BASED SERVICE TO LOCATE YOUR FAMILY ON THE MAP

TRANSPARENT TOOLBAR KEEPS THE MAP VISIBLE

INTERACTIVE MAP WITH DRAG AND ZOOM OPTIONS

LOCATING USERS IN REAL TIME AND PLOTS ON THE MAP

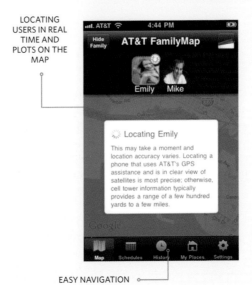

CURRENT LOCATION AND OPTION FOR CUSTOM BOOKMARKS

EASY NAVIGATION

73

Branded App

A MOBILE APP MEANT TO EXTEND A BRAND'S VALUE PROPOSITION

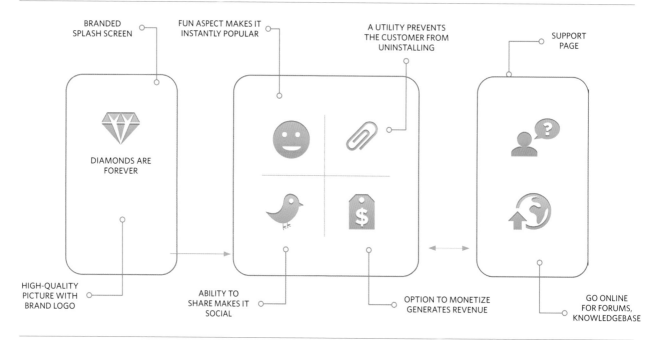

BRANDED SPLASH SCREEN

FUN ASPECT MAKES IT INSTANTLY POPULAR

A UTILITY PREVENTS THE CUSTOMER FROM UNINSTALLING

SUPPORT PAGE

DIAMONDS ARE FOREVER

HIGH-QUALITY PICTURE WITH BRAND LOGO

ABILITY TO SHARE MAKES IT SOCIAL

OPTION TO MONETIZE GENERATES REVENUE

GO ONLINE FOR FORUMS, KNOWLEDGEBASE

A mobile branded app is used for extending an existing web application or service on a mobile device. The app experience is much more immersive, providing a richer and more engaging experience. It is meant to provide utility or simple entertainment. It leverages consumers' already existing interest in the value offered by the brand's products or services.

Best Practices and Design Guidelines
- Create branded aesthetic splash screens with stunning high-quality graphics
- Keep the app simple and focused on a single utility or entertainment
- Allow for personalization and make it fun
- Add social sharing and engage user with bookmarking, reviews, and ratings
- Maintain a support screen with contact and feedback option

User Experience
- Maintain quality and usefulness
- Keep the theme and style consistent with the product/service
- Keep the data dynamic and fresh for the user to come back to the app
- Keep the basic app's functionality working in the offline mode
- Avoid marketing and advertisements; instead, sell the related product
- Leverage device's APIs to add unique experiences

(+) See also **Mobile Phone App** on page 128, **Mobile Game App** on page 144, and **Consumer Service App** on page 150.

iFood Plus

This is a meal-planning app that has a complete grocery list for every meal with recipes. The app features high-quality pictures of quick meals with recipes and a timer utility. It's one of the popular branded apps (cost is 99¢) and has great social integration. It allows the user to add ratings and reviews to each recipe.

BRANDED HIGH-QUALITY SPLASH SCREEN

SHOPPING CART INFORMATION

REGULARLY UPDATED CONTENT

DAZZLING PICTURES FOR A GREAT USER EXPERIENCE

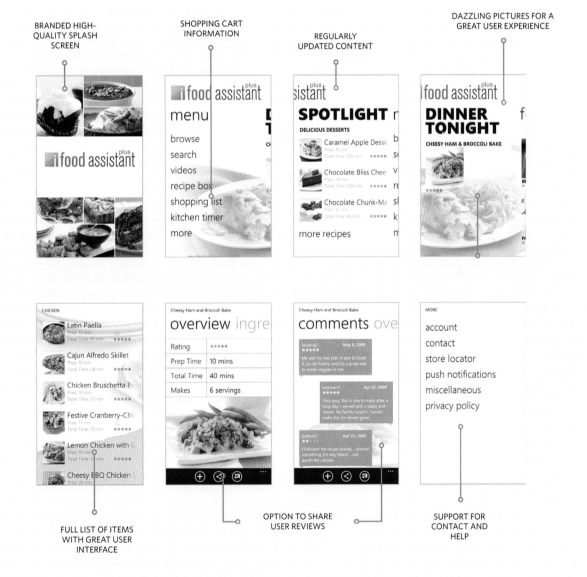

FULL LIST OF ITEMS WITH GREAT USER INTERFACE

OPTION TO SHARE USER REVIEWS

SUPPORT FOR CONTACT AND HELP

74

Consumer Service App

A NATIVE APP TO EXTEND AN ONLINE CONSUMER SERVICE

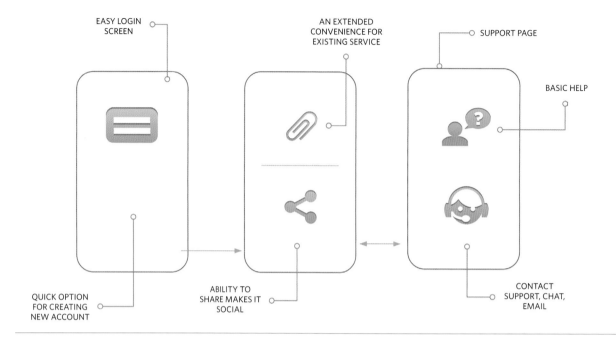

EASY LOGIN SCREEN

AN EXTENDED CONVENIENCE FOR EXISTING SERVICE

SUPPORT PAGE

BASIC HELP

QUICK OPTION FOR CREATING NEW ACCOUNT

ABILITY TO SHARE MAKES IT SOCIAL

CONTACT SUPPORT, CHAT, EMAIL

A consumer service app can be thought of as a branded app that provides extended functionality of an online service. It typically requires login and provides users with the parts of a service that are relevant in the mobile context. It's typically used for online services such as banking, project management, social networks, email, and other services that need user accounts.

Best Practices and Design Guidelines
- Keep the app straightforward for the specific service and functionality
- Make the landing page as login and save user name
- Have minimal help and allow basic functionality without login
- Assure user about security and indicate logout after the session
- Provide a separate contact and support page and allow user feedback

User Experience
- Keep the app quick and to the point
- Focus on the relevant service for mobile users
- Utilize device APIs such as GPS to minimize user input
- Allow options for auto sign-in and saving login information
- Avoid banner ads, company news, and irrelevant information

(+) See also **Mobile Phone App** on page 128 and **Branded App** on page 148.

Bank of America Mobile App

The Bank of America mobile app enables you to access your account information, transfer funds, and pay your bills (for eligible customers) from a smartphone with Internet access. It's an added convenience for existing customers. The app asks for user login and provides the most relevant features for the mobile user, such as bank and ATM locations. The app has an extensive contact support page for direct feedback, recommendations, and contact options.

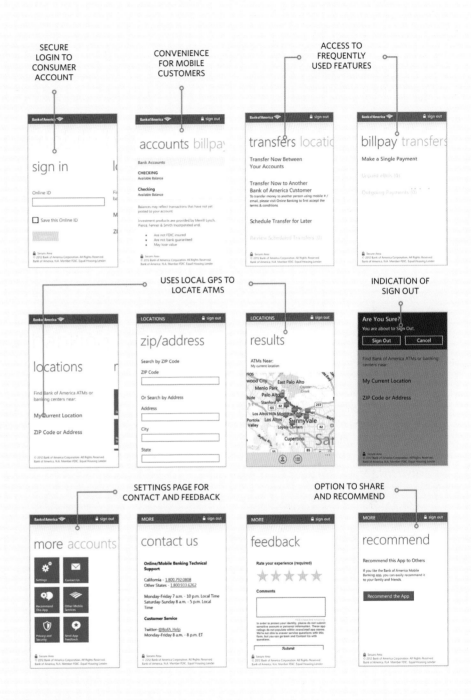

SECURE LOGIN TO CONSUMER ACCOUNT

CONVENIENCE FOR MOBILE CUSTOMERS

ACCESS TO FREQUENTLY USED FEATURES

USES LOCAL GPS TO LOCATE ATMS

INDICATION OF SIGN OUT

SETTINGS PAGE FOR CONTACT AND FEEDBACK

OPTION TO SHARE AND RECOMMEND

75

Augmented Reality App

AN APP THAT ALLOWS USERS TO INTERACT WITH THE VIRTUAL WORLD THROUGH A CAMERA LENS

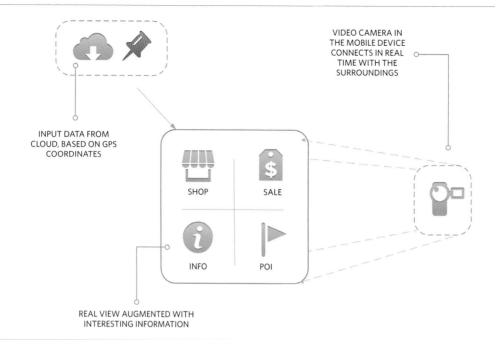

INPUT DATA FROM
CLOUD, BASED ON GPS
COORDINATES

VIDEO CAMERA IN
THE MOBILE DEVICE
CONNECTS IN REAL
TIME WITH THE
SURROUNDINGS

SHOP

SALE

INFO

POI

REAL VIEW AUGMENTED WITH
INTERESTING INFORMATION

An augmented reality app is a camera app that uses real-time image data from the camera view and processes that with information from GPS, maps, contacts, and data from the web to create an alternate virtual reality. This allows the user to navigate augmented reality in unique ways, such as interact in 3-D or find shops, places, friends, and promotions.

Best Practices and Design Guidelines
- Have camera view with transparent layers of information
- Make virtual reality on top of the real-time camera view
- Have map view and details view for using the information
- Allow interaction with the virtual world for people, places, and things
- Put the app on standby when not in use to save power and data consumption

User Experience
- Make the lens view touchable with layers of information
- Include a help function with screenshots
- Allow settings for filtering data
- Show the distance from the current location for places and people
- Allow real-time interaction, such as booking a hotel or messaging a friend

(+) See also **Camera App** on page 140 and **Location Aware App** on page 146.

Wikitude Augmented Reality App

Wikitude uses the camera and location to show interesting information in a live view. The Wikitude shows points of interest on both lens view and map view. The user is able to click/touch to get more information. Wikitude uses multiple online data sources, including Wikipedia, Yelp, Twitter, and City Search, to collect local data relevant to the user.

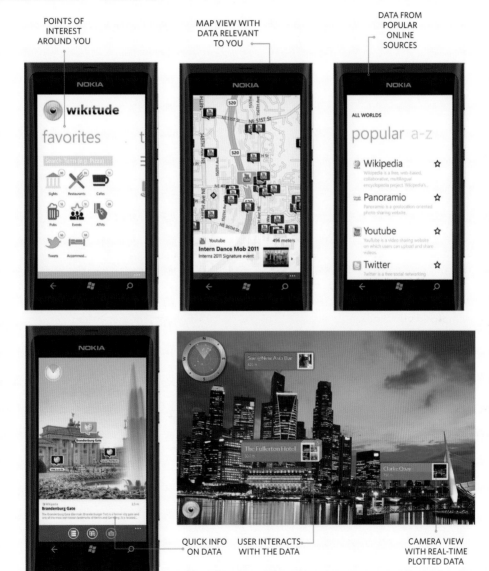

POINTS OF INTEREST AROUND YOU

MAP VIEW WITH DATA RELEVANT TO YOU

DATA FROM POPULAR ONLINE SOURCES

QUICK INFO ON DATA

USER INTERACTS WITH THE DATA

CAMERA VIEW WITH REAL-TIME PLOTTED DATA

76

Bluetooth App

A MOBILE APP UTILIZING WIRELESS BLUETOOTH TECHNOLOGY FOR COMMUNICATION

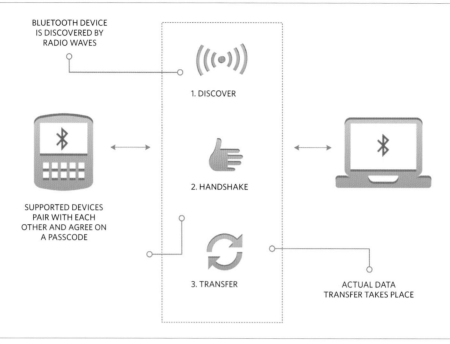

BLUETOOTH DEVICE IS DISCOVERED BY RADIO WAVES

1. DISCOVER

2. HANDSHAKE

SUPPORTED DEVICES PAIR WITH EACH OTHER AND AGREE ON A PASSCODE

3. TRANSFER

ACTUAL DATA TRANSFER TAKES PLACE

A Bluetooth mobile app allows you to communicate with other supported Bluetooth devices. Bluetooth is a simple and secure wireless technology that provides short-range communications and can be leveraged as an innovative mobile app for sharing virtual business cards and contact information, accepting social connections, making file transfers, and utilizing chat and remote control.

Best Practices and Design Guidelines

- Keep the user interface simple and easy to use for nontechnical users
- Use the device's APIs to list all Bluetooth devices in the range
- Allow permission-based pairing where both devices enter/accept the passcode
- Connect only with devices supported with Bluetooth app
- Show the status of data communication

User Experience

- Make it a quick utility with great user experience
- Do not use a splash screen
- Have quick "Bluetooth On" to list devices
- Show progress bar for large file transfer and allow bulk file transfer
- Allow sharing the Bluetooth app from within the app

(+) See also **Near Field Communication (NFC) App** on page 156 and **Mobile Phone App** on page 129.

Easy Connect for Windows 7

Easy Connect is a simple Windows Phone 7 app for accessing the Bluetooth setting in the phone quickly. A user can tap the Bluetooth icon to go to the setting to pair with other devices. Although no type of data transfer is done, the simplicity of the app shows the standard practice while developing a Bluetooth app.

EASY CONNECT APP ALLOWS YOU TO QUICKLY CONNECT TO A BLUETOOTH DEVICE

SHORTCUT TO BLUETOOTH SETTINGS

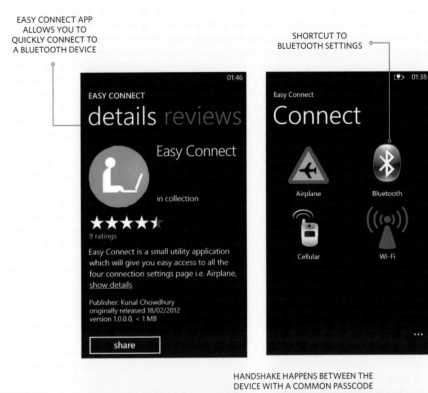

HANDSHAKE HAPPENS BETWEEN THE DEVICE WITH A COMMON PASSCODE

SWITCHING ON BLUETOOTH SETTING LISTS ALL BLUETOOTH DEVICES DISCOVERED WITHIN RANGE

ONCE DEVICE IS PAIRED, THE DATA TRANSFER TAKES PLACE BASED ON PREDEFINED PROTOCOL

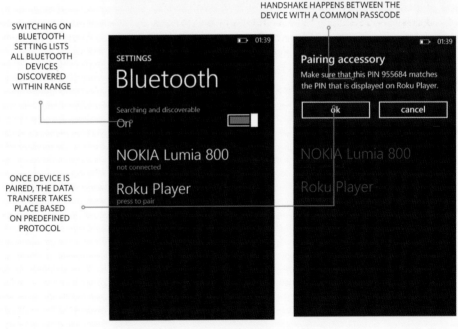

77

Near Field Communication (NFC) App

A MOBILE APP THAT USES NFC TECHNOLOGY (RADIO COMMUNICATION IN CLOSE PROXIMITY)

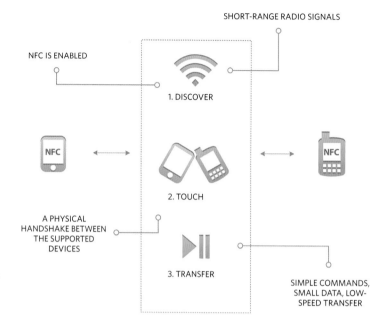

Near field communication (NFC) is a wireless technology that allows two or more devices to connect simply by physically touching them lightly. It enables two-way communication between endpoints. Unlike Bluetooth wireless technology, where the pairing of the two devices is required using a passcode, NFC technology automatically pairs two devices when they are in close proximity to each other. It's a low-speed connection with a simple setup.

Best Practices and Design Guidelines

- Have a setting to confirm sharing and connecting
- Have a simple screen for action progress on device touch
- There are no additional steps, so the app sends/receives commands on touch
- Use a simple on/off setting screen for NFC
- Use standard protocols for both devices
- NFC allows both one-way and two-way communication between the devices

User Experience

- Keep the app quick and to the point
- Have innovative ways of sharing, getting phone numbers on touch, and connecting to social networks
- Show progress when transferring data

(+) See also **Bluetooth App** on page 154 and **Mobile Phone App** on page 128.

Nokia N9 and NFC Speakers

Nokia was one of the first companies to come up with NFC-enabled phones. The latest N9 features a unique music app that allows it to connect NFC-enabled speakers. If you're out listening to a song and come home, you can transfer the music from your phone's speakers to the house speakers simply by touching them. When leaving, use the phone to touch the home speakers again and the song is back playing on the phone.

NOKIA N9 MUSIC
APP USES NFC
TECHNOLOGY

NFC-ENABLED
SPEAKERS

NFC BOOTS UP
THE BLUETOOTH
CONNECTION, WHICH
THEN TRANSFERS THE
MUSIC

ON TOUCH, THE SONG
IS TRANSFERED FROM
PHONE TO SPEAKER
AND BACK

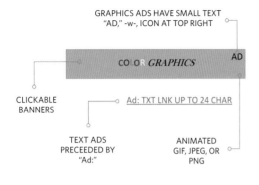

GRAPHICS ADS HAVE SMALL TEXT
"AD," -w-, ICON AT TOP RIGHT

COLOR *GRAPHICS*   AD

CLICKABLE
BANNERS

Ad: TXT LNK UP TO 24 CHAR

TEXT ADS
PRECEEDED BY
"Ad:"

ANIMATED
GIF, JPEG, OR
PNG

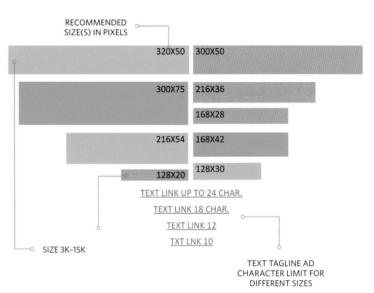

RECOMMENDED
SIZE(S) IN PIXELS

320X50	300X50	
300X75	216X36	
	168X28	
216X54	168X42	
128X20	128X30	

TEXT LINK UP TO 24 CHAR.

TEXT LINK 18 CHAR.

TEXT LINK 12

TXT LNK 10

SIZE 3K–15K

TEXT TAGLINE AD
CHARACTER LIMIT FOR
DIFFERENT SIZES

There are three kinds of mobile ads: a graphic banner ad; a text-based ad; and a full-screen, media-rich ad. The banner ads and text ads are more popular and are used on mobile websites as well as mobile apps. A full-screen, media-rich app is generally part of a mobile app or media app that gets triggered either by users clicking on the existing banner or in a video playback.

Best Practices and Design Guidelines

- Keep the ad clearly separated from the content or label it as an ad
- Includes the word "ad" in the top-right or bottom-right corner
- For text ads, use advertising indicators "ad:" or "-w-"
- Use dimensions ranging from 128 × 20 pixels to 320 × 50 pixels
- Use recommended size of 3K up to 15K, with file type JPEG, PNG, or GIF
- Have text banners range from small (10 characters) to large (24 characters)
- For full-screen, media-rich ads, videos should be 30 or fewer seconds

User Experience

- Keep ads relevant and fast loading
- Use optimized images for fast loading
- Keep banner ads to a maximum of two lines of text
- Avoid using rich Internet applications such as Flash or Silverlight
- Leverage device's geolocation to serve local ads

(+) See also **Web Widget** on page 98, **Banner Ad** on page 102, and **Rich Internet Application (RIA)** on page 96.

m.imdb.com (N9), Quick Scan, and Convert Units

The mobile website m.imdb.com features a graphics banner ad that is clearly separated from the website at the top of the page. The Quick Scan app features a graphically aesthetic ad with 100 percent width, whereas Convert Units shows a text-based ad that rotates text at the top of the app.

GRAPHIC AD IN IMDB WEBSITE CLEARLY SEPARATED FROM THE CONTENT

TEXT AD INSIDE THE CONTENT WITH THE TOP-RIGHT AD MESSAGE

AD THEME MATCHES THE APP BUT CLEARLY SAYS "AdChoices"

IN-APP BANNER AD

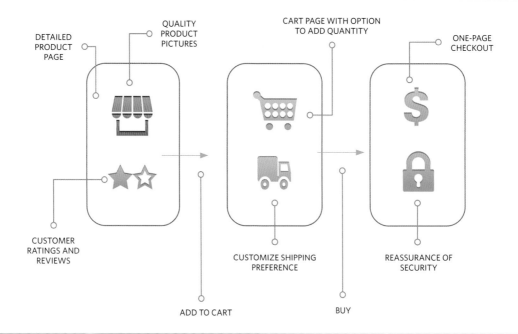

DETAILED PRODUCT PAGE

QUALITY PRODUCT PICTURES

CART PAGE WITH OPTION TO ADD QUANTITY

ONE-PAGE CHECKOUT

CUSTOMER RATINGS AND REVIEWS

CUSTOMIZE SHIPPING PREFERENCE

REASSURANCE OF SECURITY

ADD TO CART

BUY

Mobile commerce is an essential and simplified version of e-commerce on the web. The first step in mobile commerce is the product detail page. Customers spend most of their time on this page deciding whether to buy the product or pass. The next page is Add to Cart, which allows users to add and remove quantities. The third and final step is the checkout, where users either login and reuse existing information or enter billing and shipping details to buy the product.

Best Practices and Design Guidelines
- Have a detailed product page with quality pictures, specifications, and reviews
- Keep good-quality pictures but optimize for size
- Keep minimum number of steps—ideally three for mobile commerce
- Save user preferences, such as items added to cart and login information, for returning customers
- Keep a white background with minimal theme and style

User Experience
- Avoid banner ads and promotions
- Allow user to simply check out with option to log in
- Assure user of security during checkout
- Keep the pages scrolling vertically on a mobile device
- Have an option to go to the desktop version

(+) See also **Shopping Cart** on page 70, **Product Page** on page 68, and **Checkout** on page 72.

Infibeam is an Indian mobile shopping website featuring a simple and straightforward mobile commerce experience. The product detail page lists all the details of the product with complete specifications and warranty information. The shopping cart allows users to check out as new customers. In the very final step, it asks for bank or credit card information for purchase.

PRODUCT DETAIL PAGE WITH PICTURES, PRICE, AND COLOR OPTIONS

OTHER SPECIFICATIONS AND WARRANTY INFORMATION

SHOPPING CART WITH UPDATED QUANTITY

CHECK OUT AS NEW CUSTOMER

FINAL STEP FOR CHECKOUT

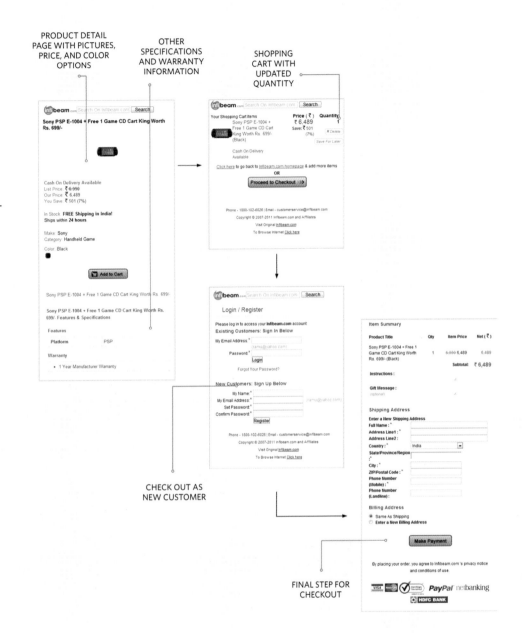

80

Mobile Search

A SEARCH USER INTERFACE FOR MOBILE DEVICES

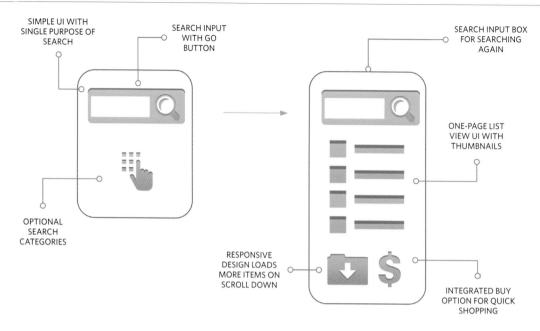

SIMPLE UI WITH SINGLE PURPOSE OF SEARCH

SEARCH INPUT WITH GO BUTTON

SEARCH INPUT BOX FOR SEARCHING AGAIN

ONE-PAGE LIST VIEW UI WITH THUMBNAILS

OPTIONAL SEARCH CATEGORIES

RESPONSIVE DESIGN LOADS MORE ITEMS ON SCROLL DOWN

INTEGRATED BUY OPTION FOR QUICK SHOPPING

A mobile search is a great example of a focused mobile app: the user types a keyword, optionally selects a subcategory, presses Go, and a list of relevant items is shown. The user can further search or select one of the items or scroll down, which loads more items. The search result may even have an Add to Cart option for quick e-commerce.

Best Practices and Design Guidelines

- Have search screen with optional categories
- Show thumbnails in the search result list page
- Use white background with clear two- or three-color theme for the search results page
- For online shopping websites, have Buy option in the results page
- Use simple text buttons such as Buy and Go instead of Add to Cart and Search
- Load more items with vertical scroll instead of using multiple pages and navigation

User Experience

- Keep it easy to use with quick results
- Have big, tappable buttons
- Allow readable search input box
- Have precise and accessible content
- Use two or three colors with white background

(+) See also **Information App** on page 132 and **Branded App** on page 148.

Apmex is a gold dealer that has its own mobile website. The website features a simple search along with the categories for browsing. The search results page has a list view with thumbnails and navigation-based paging mechanisms instead of responsive design.

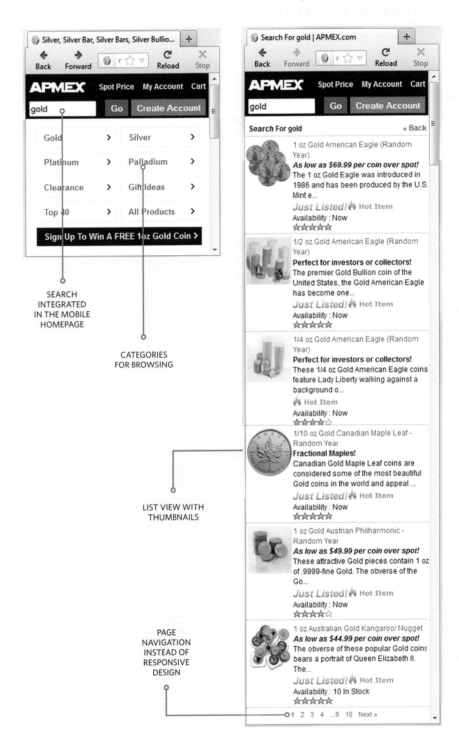

SEARCH
INTEGRATED
IN THE MOBILE
HOMEPAGE

CATEGORIES
FOR BROWSING

LIST VIEW WITH
THUMBNAILS

PAGE
NAVIGATION
INSTEAD OF
RESPONSIVE
DESIGN

81

Mobile Home Screen

LANDING SCREEN FOR A MOBILE DEVICE

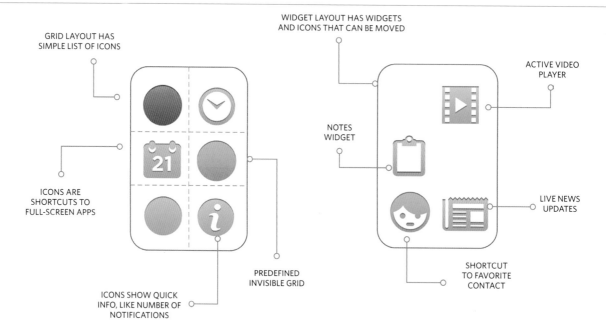

WIDGET LAYOUT HAS WIDGETS
AND ICONS THAT CAN BE MOVED

GRID LAYOUT HAS
SIMPLE LIST OF ICONS

ACTIVE VIDEO
PLAYER

NOTES
WIDGET

ICONS ARE
SHORTCUTS TO
FULL-SCREEN APPS

LIVE NEWS
UPDATES

PREDEFINED
INVISIBLE GRID

SHORTCUT
TO FAVORITE
CONTACT

ICONS SHOW QUICK
INFO, LIKE NUMBER OF
NOTIFICATIONS

A mobile home screen is the first screen users see after unlocking the device. It is meant to help users find their way to apps and settings. There are two popular home screen layouts. One is the icon grid pattern, where you have a number of static and interactive icons. This pattern is popular with iPhone and the Windows phone. The other layout is a customizable widget pattern that allows users to have a live widget on the home screen. This layout is popularly used in Symbian and Android phones.

Best Practices and Design Guidelines
- Allow quick access to frequently used apps
- Allow easy access to all apps and settings in the phone
- Optimize icons for display
- Have simple interaction from home screen to app
- Allow customization of home screen

User Experience
- Have everything easily accessible
- Create big tappable icons and buttons
- Have ability to remove, move around, and change the layout
- Use multiple screens to group icons and widgets

(+) See also **Touch User Interface** on page 166 and **Homepage** on page 54.

For its N9, Nokia has come up with a different and innovative layout with three screens for the homepage that can be swiped left to right like a carousel. The first screen is a notification screen, the second is an icon grid, and the third is for recently used applications. It's an innovative approach to mobile home screen design.

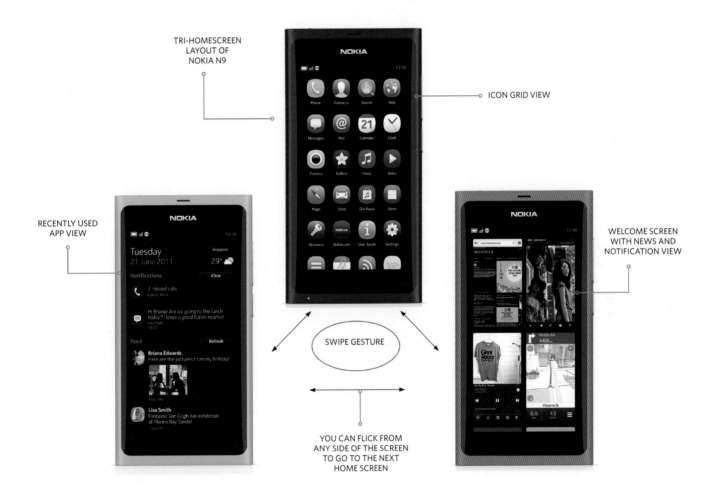

TRI-HOMESCREEN
LAYOUT OF
NOKIA N9

ICON GRID VIEW

RECENTLY USED
APP VIEW

WELCOME SCREEN
WITH NEWS AND
NOTIFICATION VIEW

SWIPE GESTURE

YOU CAN FLICK FROM
ANY SIDE OF THE SCREEN
TO GO TO THE NEXT
HOME SCREEN

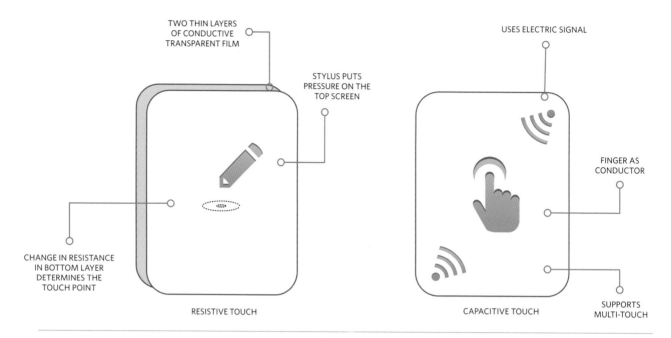

TWO THIN LAYERS OF CONDUCTIVE TRANSPARENT FILM

STYLUS PUTS PRESSURE ON THE TOP SCREEN

CHANGE IN RESISTANCE IN BOTTOM LAYER DETERMINES THE TOUCH POINT

RESISTIVE TOUCH

USES ELECTRIC SIGNAL

FINGER AS CONDUCTOR

SUPPORTS MULTI-TOUCH

CAPACITIVE TOUCH

A touch user interface is created using haptics, a technology that uses tactile feedback on a hardware surface to sense touch. The two implementations are resistive touch and capacitive touch. Resistive touch uses pressure to locate the focus point of the touch. Capacitive touch uses electric signals and is suitable for multi-touch.

Best Practices and Design Guidelines
- For resistive touch
  - Use single-touch interaction with stylus accuracy
  - Don't allow dragging
  - Use paging instead of scrolling
  - Use fixed-sized buttons for interaction
- For capacitive touch
  - Have smooth interaction using finger touch
  - Have smooth scrolling behavior to support dragging
  - Allow interacting with the content
  - Have multi-touch for advanced features

User Experience
- Create a seamless interaction; trade off features for better experience
- Use fluid, smooth scrolling on a capacitive screen
- For resistive screen, use definite interaction—point-and-click-like behavior

(+) See also **Multi-Touch User Interface** on page 168 and **Gesture-Based User Interface** on page 10.

One-Touch User Interface

This concept, built for a capacitive touch screen, uses drag-like flick gestures to move in or out of the application menu. You can interact with a touch screen device with one touch (single point of interaction), and you can flick to interact with the user interface without lifting a finger.

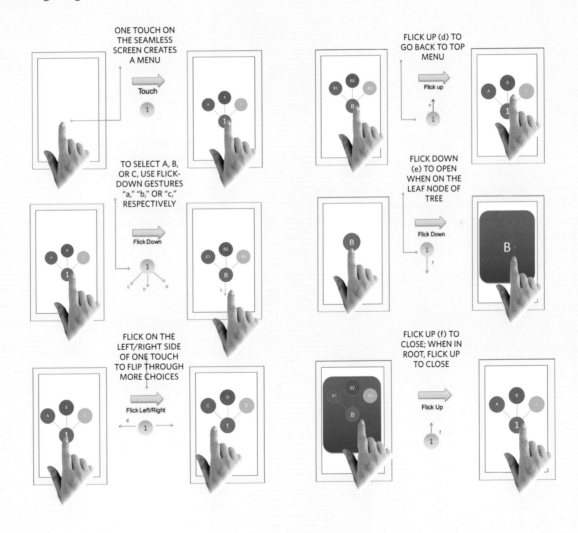

ONE TOUCH ON THE SEAMLESS SCREEN CREATES A MENU

Touch

TO SELECT A, B, OR C, USE FLICK-DOWN GESTURES "a," "b," OR "c," RESPECTIVELY

Flick Down

FLICK ON THE LEFT/RIGHT SIDE OF ONE TOUCH TO FLIP THROUGH MORE CHOICES

Flick Left/Right

FLICK UP (d) TO GO BACK TO TOP MENU

Flick up

FLICK DOWN (e) TO OPEN WHEN ON THE LEAF NODE OF TREE

Flick Down

FLICK UP (f) TO CLOSE; WHEN IN ROOT, FLICK UP TO CLOSE

Flick Up

83

Multi-Touch User Interface

A USER INTERFACE THAT ALLOWS FOR MULTIPLE, SIMULTANEOUS TOUCH INPUTS

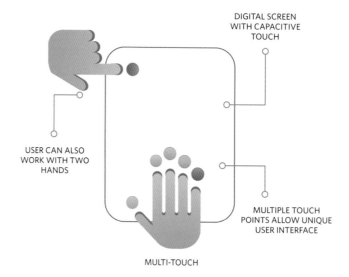

DIGITAL SCREEN
WITH CAPACITIVE
TOUCH

USER CAN ALSO
WORK WITH TWO
HANDS

MULTIPLE TOUCH
POINTS ALLOW UNIQUE
USER INTERFACE

MULTI-TOUCH

Multi-touch uses a digital screen that recognizes two or more points of contact on the surface concurrently. It tracks the multiple points, allowing the interface to recognize gestures. This enables advanced functionality, such as flick, pinch-to-zoom, and more. Multi-touch uses capacitive touch screen technology for input.

Best Practices and Design Guidelines
- Innovate on simple user interaction
- Think logical for two-hand interaction
- Use simple flick gestures
    - Drag left, right, top, and down
    - Rotate, pinch in, and pinch out
    - Tap, double tap
- Have input-based interface, where user touches one point to open submenu

User Experience
- Use the fewest number of touch points (two or three) for interaction
- Avoid awkward interaction with multiple fingers
- Don't allow for ten-finger input just because you can
- Have innovative user experiences, which delights users

(+) See also **Touch User Interface** on page 166 and **Gesture-Based User Interface** on page 171.

Two Thumbs User Interface

This is a user concept utilizing multiple inputs to interact with a digital photo frame. It allows for an unobtrusive view, and is best suited for two thumbs interaction. It uses a unique tree menu, where each menu item is in a rotating dial interface on the left side with a submenu on the right. The two thumbs interface uses multi-touch in a unique and effective way.

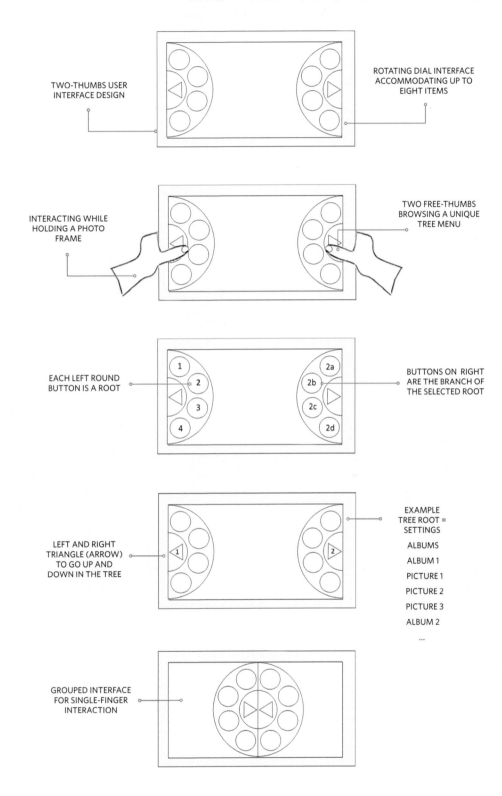

TWO-THUMBS USER INTERFACE DESIGN

ROTATING DIAL INTERFACE ACCOMMODATING UP TO EIGHT ITEMS

INTERACTING WHILE HOLDING A PHOTO FRAME

TWO FREE-THUMBS BROWSING A UNIQUE TREE MENU

EACH LEFT ROUND BUTTON IS A ROOT

BUTTONS ON RIGHT ARE THE BRANCH OF THE SELECTED ROOT

LEFT AND RIGHT TRIANGLE (ARROW) TO GO UP AND DOWN IN THE TREE

EXAMPLE
TREE ROOT = SETTINGS

ALBUMS

ALBUM 1

PICTURE 1

PICTURE 2

PICTURE 3

ALBUM 2

...

GROUPED INTERFACE FOR SINGLE-FINGER INTERACTION

84

Accessible Touch User Interface

AN ACCESSIBLE INTERFACE FOR A TOUCH SCREEN

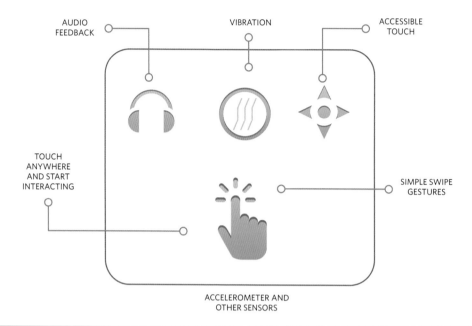

An accessible interface made for a touch screen device uses simple touch-based interaction, audio, haptic feedback (vibration), accelerometer, and other sensor technologies. Due to the lack of a tactile surface, it's difficult for a touch screen to create a Braille interface for the visually impaired. Other current solutions include screen readers, voice-recognition systems, and voice commands.

Best Practices and Design Guidelines

- Have the interface tailored for accessibility
- Have feedback at each step using audio and vibrations
- Use accelerometer and other sensors to support interaction
- Design the UI with a limited number of easy gestures

User Experience

- Target extreme simplicity and accuracy
- Use basic interaction
- Always announce context
- Use vibrations sparingly
- Use advanced sensors such as accelerometer to help interaction

+ See also **Touch User Interface** on page 166 and **Gesture-Based User Interface** on page 171, and **Multi-Touch User Interface** on page 168.

Tap Interface

This UI concept for the visually impaired uses an interaction based on Morse code. The user taps on the device to interact. The device interacts back in the form of vibrations (haptic feedback) and audio. The interface can be easily adapted for simplistic mobile devices, emergency calls in existing phones, MP3 players, radios, and remote controls.

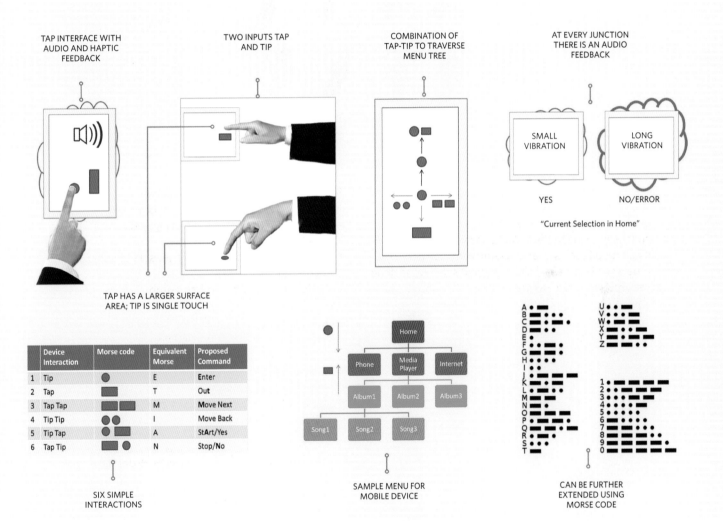

TAP INTERFACE WITH
AUDIO AND HAPTIC
FEEDBACK

TWO INPUTS TAP
AND TIP

COMBINATION OF
TAP-TIP TO TRAVERSE
MENU TREE

AT EVERY JUNCTION
THERE IS AN AUDIO
FEEDBACK

SMALL VIBRATION — YES

LONG VIBRATION — NO/ERROR

"Current Selection in Home"

TAP HAS A LARGER SURFACE
AREA; TIP IS SINGLE TOUCH

	Device Interaction	Morse code	Equivalent Morse	Proposed Command
1	Tip	●	E	Enter
2	Tap	▬	T	Out
3	Tap Tap	▬ ▬	M	Move Next
4	Tip Tip	● ●	I	Move Back
5	Tip Tap	● ▬	A	StArt/Yes
6	Tap Tip	▬ ●	N	Stop/No

SIX SIMPLE
INTERACTIONS

SAMPLE MENU FOR
MOBILE DEVICE

CAN BE FURTHER
EXTENDED USING
MORSE CODE

Gesture-Based User Interface

AN INTERFACE UTILIZING TOUCH GESTURES TO INTERACT

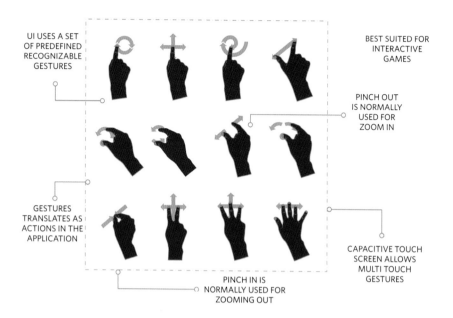

UI USES A SET OF PREDEFINED RECOGNIZABLE GESTURES

BEST SUITED FOR INTERACTIVE GAMES

PINCH OUT IS NORMALLY USED FOR ZOOM IN

GESTURES TRANSLATES AS ACTIONS IN THE APPLICATION

CAPACITIVE TOUCH SCREEN ALLOWS MULTI TOUCH GESTURES

PINCH IN IS NORMALLY USED FOR ZOOMING OUT

This type of interface is made up of simple, recognizable gestures using one, two, or more fingers, where the user drags and creates symbols on the touch screen and the interface translates them into a standard command for the application. For example, a cross sign made by a finger can be translated as a delete action inside an application. Gesture-based user interfaces are very popular among interactive teaching apps and games.

Best Practices and Design Guidelines
- Have a set of predefined gestures for commands
- Give feedback on the command translation
- Help user interact with the app
- Specify a particular block of screen for gestures
- Have quick help on interactions like a control panel for games

User expectation from a gesture-based UI is interactivity.

User Experience
- Keep it simple and fun
- Allow user to learn while interacting
- Use standard and familiar gestures, such as pinch out for zoom
- Use simple, recognizable gestures

(+) See also **Touch User Interface** on page 166 and **Multi-Touch User Interface** on page 168, and **Pen-Based Interface** on page 173

Pen-Based Interface

AN INTERFACE USING STYLUS-BASED INPUT

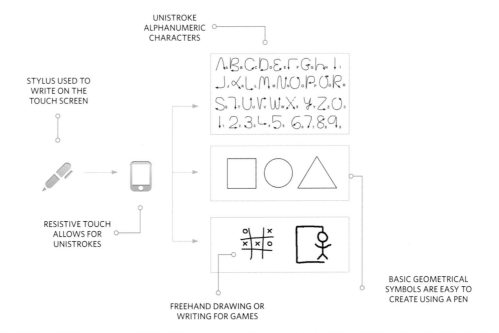

UNISTROKE
ALPHANUMERIC
CHARACTERS

STYLUS USED TO
WRITE ON THE
TOUCH SCREEN

RESISTIVE TOUCH
ALLOWS FOR
UNISTROKES

FREEHAND DRAWING OR
WRITING FOR GAMES

BASIC GEOMETRICAL
SYMBOLS ARE EASY TO
CREATE USING A PEN

A pen-based interface uses a virtual pen to interact. Pen-based interfaces have been around since the earliest handheld devices and used stylus strokes on resistive touch screens to write. Modern capacitive touch screens can also simulate stylus-like behavior using conductor pens or finger touches. They are used for three types of applications: inputting text using handwriting recognition, also known as graffiti input; creating basic shapes and symbols; and drawing on the screen.

Best Practices and Design Guidelines
- Have auto-suggest feature for text input
- Teach users while they draw
- Show suggestions and possible output characters
- For games, map simple strokes to commands
- Allow a particular area in the interface for input

User Experience
- Use for quick utility such as note taking and fun drawing
- Use fuzzy logic to approximate shape
- Allow application to learn user input
- Have a forgiving interface with undo option
- Have auto-correction feature

(+) See also **Gesture-Based User Interface** on page 172 and **Touch User Interface** on page 166.

Mobile Clock App

A CLOCK UTILITY FOR MOBILE APPLICATIONS

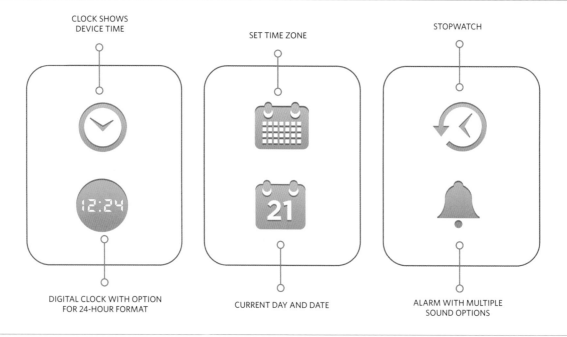

CLOCK SHOWS DEVICE TIME

SET TIME ZONE

STOPWATCH

DIGITAL CLOCK WITH OPTION FOR 24-HOUR FORMAT

CURRENT DAY AND DATE

ALARM WITH MULTIPLE SOUND OPTIONS

A mobile clock is an application that mimics a traditional clock. It takes time data from the device and shows it in either digital format or as an analog clock. It features a number of related functionalities, including multiple time zones for different cities around the world, a stopwatch, and an alarm.

Best Practices and Design Guidelines
- Keep the design unique, useful, and aesthetic
- Allow for easy settings of time zone, alarms, etc
- Have settings for alarms and multiple sound types
- Format clock according to the target user
  - Sports clock may need milliseconds display
  - Artists may prefer analog clock with no numbers
  - Utility-based clock for stopwatch, world clock, etc

User Experience
- Create a clock that is easy to use and great to look at
- Provide large size for time display
- Keep the clock display simple and clear
- Have proper contrast between hour/minute hands and the background

(+) See also **World Clock App** on page 176 and **Information App** on page 132.

Colour Clock Concept

The Colour Clock is an aesthetic clock concept that changes color and sets the ambience based on the time of day. It provides a visual cue for the time and, because of the distinct color, a user can tell the time within a two-hour range just by looking at the color. The clock uses a twelve-color wheel to create a unique aesthetic experience for the viewer. It uses contrasting colors for the background and the dial at any particular instance.

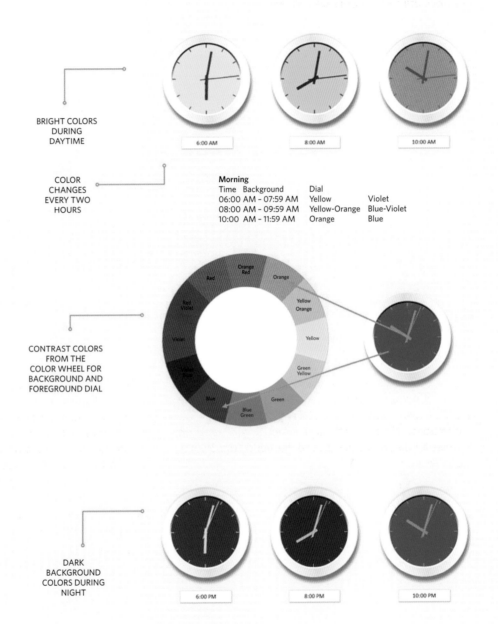

BRIGHT COLORS DURING DAYTIME

COLOR CHANGES EVERY TWO HOURS

CONTRAST COLORS FROM THE COLOR WHEEL FOR BACKGROUND AND FOREGROUND DIAL

DARK BACKGROUND COLORS DURING NIGHT

6:00 AM 8:00 AM 10:00 AM

Morning

Time	Background	Dial
06:00 AM – 07:59 AM	Yellow	Violet
08:00 AM – 09:59 AM	Yellow-Orange	Blue-Violet
10:00 AM – 11:59 AM	Orange	Blue

6:00 PM 8:00 PM 10:00 PM

88

World Clock App

A CLOCK APP THAT SHOWS THE TIME FOR MULTIPLE CITIES

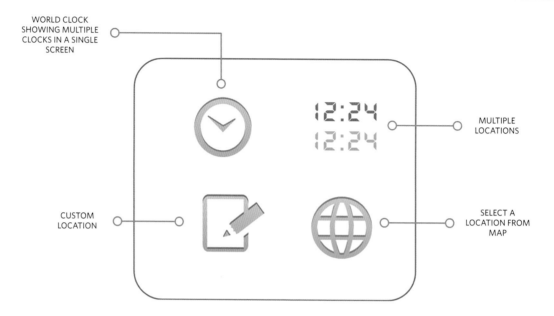

WORLD CLOCK SHOWING MULTIPLE CLOCKS IN A SINGLE SCREEN

MULTIPLE LOCATIONS

CUSTOM LOCATION

SELECT A LOCATION FROM MAP

A world clock is a special kind of clock that shows time zones for multiple cities at the same time. It is a handy tool for travelers and global teams. Instead of using multiple clock apps for multiple locations, a world clock app shows multiple time units in a single screen.

Best Practices and Design Guidelines
- Have a single screen display multiple times and cities
- Allow user to select a time zone from a list or a location from a map
- Save user preferences of cities
- Allow for daylight savings time change

User Experience
- Have simple and clear display of city and time
- Allow for customization

(+) See also **Information App** on page 132 and **Mobile Clock App** on page 174.

Mobile World Clock and New World Clock Concepts

Mobile World Clock has a single screen display time for a list of cities. New World Clock shows the time for twenty-four cities around the world. The location of the city in the clock shows the time in hours for that city. The minute is shown on the minute dial. World Clock groups and plots two cities that are on a twelve-hour time difference at the same place, one above the other. Nighttime city title is dark and daytime is light. The hour dial points to the default city. The city dial moves every hour, moving all cities to their respective time.

SINGLE SCREEN SHOWING MULTIPLE CLOCKS IN DIGITAL FORMAT

CLICK TO SELECT A LOCATION FROM THE MAP

S.	Location A	TimeZone A	Time	PM/AM	Time	TimeZone B	Location B
1	London	UTC	12:00	PM/AM	00:00	UTC+12	New Zealand
2	Cape Verde	UTC-1	11:00	AM/PM	23:00	UTC+11	Kamchatka
3	Georgia	UTC-2	10:00	AM/PM	22:00	UTC+10	Sydney
4	Argentina	UTC-3	9:00	AM/PM	21:00	UTC+9	Tokyo
5	Puerto Rico	UTC-4	8:00	AM/PM	20:00	UTC+8	Singapore
6	New York	UTC-5	7:00	AM/PM	19:00	UTC+7	Thailand
7	Mexico	UTC-6	6:00	AM/PM	18:00	UTC+6	Bangladesh
8	Arizona	UTC-7	5:00	AM/PM	17:00	UTC+5	Maldives
9	Los Angeles	UTC-8	4:00	AM/PM	16:00	UTC+4	Mauritius
10	Fairbanks	UTC-9	3:00	AM/PM	15:00	UTC+3	Moscow
11	Hawaii	UTC-10	2:00	AM/PM	14:00	UTC+2	Finland
12	Samoa	UTC-11	1:00	AM/PM	13:00	UTC+1	Germany

COORDINATED UNIVERSAL TIME (UTC) FOR 24 CITIES AROUND THE CLOCK

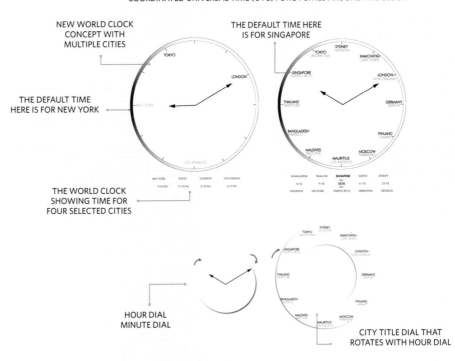

NEW WORLD CLOCK CONCEPT WITH MULTIPLE CITIES

THE DEFAULT TIME HERE IS FOR SINGAPORE

THE DEFAULT TIME HERE IS FOR NEW YORK

THE WORLD CLOCK SHOWING TIME FOR FOUR SELECTED CITIES

HOUR DIAL MINUTE DIAL

CITY TITLE DIAL THAT ROTATES WITH HOUR DIAL

89

Mashup App

A WEB APP THAT COMBINES DATA FROM MORE THAN ONE WEBSITE

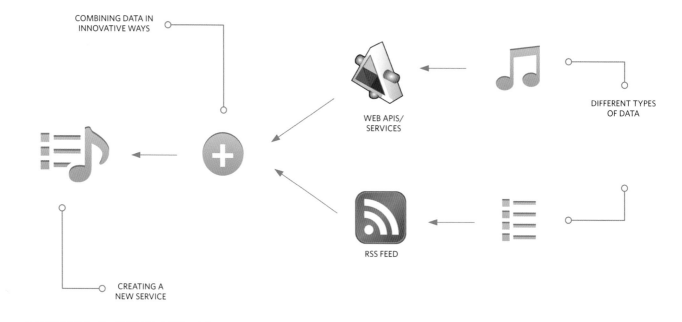

A mashup app uses web APIs of online services to mix data and functionality in a unique and innovative way to create new services. A number of mashups use a map for plotting remote data, for example, pricing data on gasoline on top of a map service to find the lowest gas prices near you.

Best Practices and Design Guidelines
- Have a single-purpose, focused application
- Allow gathering of real-time data from disparate sources
- Have option to personalize data for the user
- Have customization option based on user preferences
- Use a common UI to showcase the combined data

User Experience
- Create a new and personal experience
- Associate data with the user
- Show something dynamic and interesting
- Keep the app responsive

(+) See also **Ajax Web Application** on page 114 and **Service-Oriented Architecture (SOA) Design** on page 122.

Tastebuds.fm

A music, dating, and social network for music lovers, Tastebuds.fm is a simple mashup app with the unique idea that people with similar music choices could "connect" with each other. It uses web APIs from Last.fm to search for artists, albums, songs, etc, and matches people with similar interests. It also uses Facebook login API to integrate with the social network.

A DATING MASHUP APP BASED ON LAST.FM APIS AND FACEBOOK APIS

ADD YOUR MUSIC INTEREST TO CONNECT WITH LIKE-MINDED PEOPLE

USES FACEBOOK LOGIN APIS

TASTEBUD.FM GIVES SOCIAL NETWORK EXPERIENCE AMONG ALL YOUR POTENTIAL DATES

TASTEBUD.FM MATCHES YOUR INTERESTS WITH PEOPLE

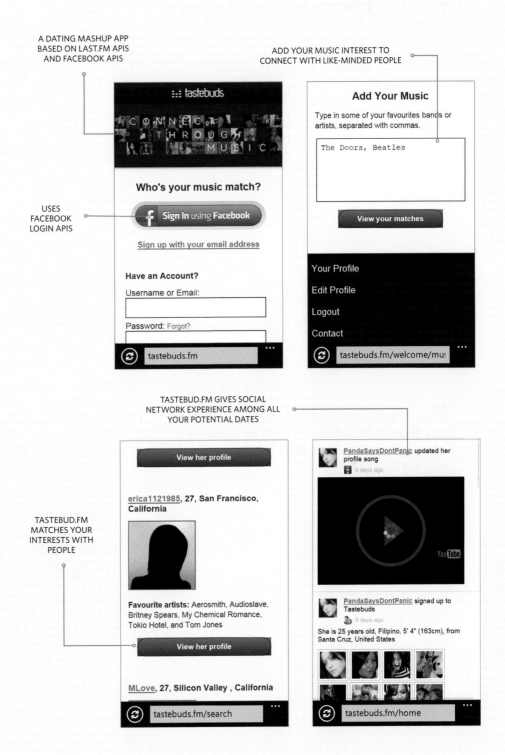

90

Voice User Interface

AN INTERFACE TO A SPEECH-BASED APPLICATION

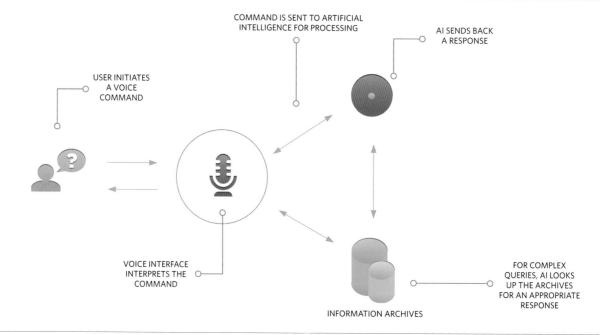

COMMAND IS SENT TO ARTIFICIAL
INTELLIGENCE FOR PROCESSING

AI SENDS BACK
A RESPONSE

USER INITIATES
A VOICE
COMMAND

VOICE INTERFACE
INTERPRETS THE
COMMAND

FOR COMPLEX
QUERIES, AI LOOKS
UP THE ARCHIVES
FOR AN APPROPRIATE
RESPONSE

INFORMATION ARCHIVES

A voice user interface allows users to interact with a speech application in an efficient way. The speech application is made of multiple components, including voice-to-text conversion, artificial intelligence, and archives of information. These all work together to formulate an easy-to-understand response for the user. Voice user interface is commonly used in computer games, mobile commands, and search functions.

Best Practices and Design Guidelines
- Have a simple, clutter-free user interface for voice input
- Perfect most commonly used commands
- Use the context for the voice commands
- Show the user voice-to-text conversion
- Give visual feedback on listening mode
- Have a two-way dialogue with user to refine the result

User Experience
- Target for assisting users with the most-accurate interpretation
- Make it easy to use with simple and concise commands
- Allow refining of result
- Try for a hands-free experience

(+) See also **Interactive Voice Response (IVR) System** on page 38 and **Mobile Phone App** on page 128.

Voice User Interface in Lumia 900

The Lumia 900 phone comes with a voice user interface that allows users to speak to the phone for quick commands and search functions. A long press on the Windows button activates the voice user interface, which shows some basic examples of voice commands and initiates the voice input when the user clicks on the Speak button. The voice is then converted into text and the appropriate command is activated.

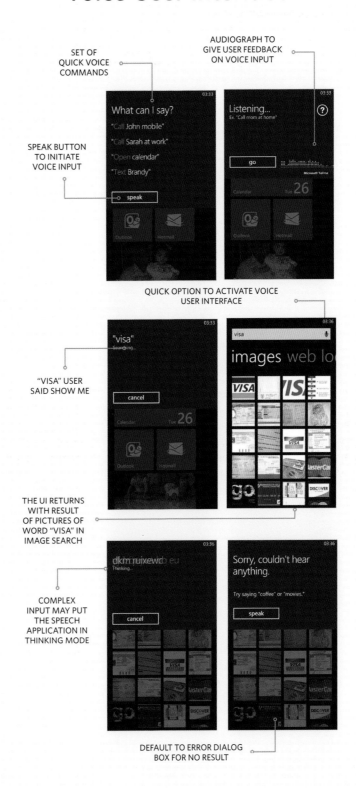

SET OF QUICK VOICE COMMANDS

AUDIOGRAPH TO GIVE USER FEEDBACK ON VOICE INPUT

SPEAK BUTTON TO INITIATE VOICE INPUT

QUICK OPTION TO ACTIVATE VOICE USER INTERFACE

"VISA" USER SAID SHOW ME

THE UI RETURNS WITH RESULT OF PICTURES OF WORD "VISA" IN IMAGE SEARCH

COMPLEX INPUT MAY PUT THE SPEECH APPLICATION IN THINKING MODE

DEFAULT TO ERROR DIALOG BOX FOR NO RESULT

91 10-Foot User Interface

A USER INTERFACE FOR LARGE-SCREEN TELEVISIONS

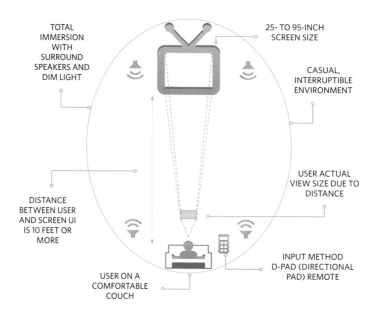

TOTAL IMMERSION WITH SURROUND SPEAKERS AND DIM LIGHT

25- TO 95-INCH SCREEN SIZE

CASUAL, INTERRUPTIBLE ENVIRONMENT

USER ACTUAL VIEW SIZE DUE TO DISTANCE

DISTANCE BETWEEN USER AND SCREEN UI IS 10 FEET OR MORE

USER ON A COMFORTABLE COUCH

INPUT METHOD D-PAD (DIRECTIONAL PAD) REMOTE

A 10-foot user interface helps you interact with a television using a remote input. The large distance between the television and the user requires a careful design, unlike computers or mobile devices, where the distance is 1 to 2 feet.

Best Practices and Design Guidelines

- Use full-screen UI for total immersion with horizontal page scrolling
- Use high-quality scalable vector graphics
- Utilize aspect ratio 4:3 or 16:9 and use high-definition 720P/1080P
- Avoid paragraphs of text—use single-line headings for titles and captions
- Use large anti-aliased sans serif fonts with minimum size of 18 points on 720P and 24 points on 1080P
- Use dark colors for fonts, which are more readable on the television, and avoid bright colors
- Have lines with a minimum of 2 points thickness and a 1-inch margin between text, images, etc

User Experience

- Use multimedia-type controls on television, such as rewind, forward, fast forward, and pause
- For total immersion, use darker background, which emits less light and is easy on the eyes
- Avoid complex interactions, touch screens, mouse, or keyboard-based entry
- Use visual cues and update user when loading dynamic content

(+) See also **Dashboard/Scorecards** on page 32 and **Rich Internet Application (RIA)** on page 96.

YuppTV Channel

YuppTV in Roku player is an Internet television channel. The user interface has a simple and user-friendly 10-foot interface for playing content.

BIG DISPLAY FOR EASY VIEWING WITH PLENTY OF EMPTY SPACE

SIMPLE AND USER-FRIENDLY INTERFACE

CAROUSEL VIEW GREAT FOR D-PAD STYLE NAVIGATION

LARGE HIGH-QUALITY IMAGE BLOCK WITH GRADIENTS AND SHADOW EFFECTS

HARDWARE STATUS OVERLAPPING THE UI

DEFAULT DARK BACKGROUND IS EASY ON EYES

STATUS OF DYNAMIC CONTENT LOADING

FOUR STARS MEANS QUALITY OF CONTENT IS 1080P

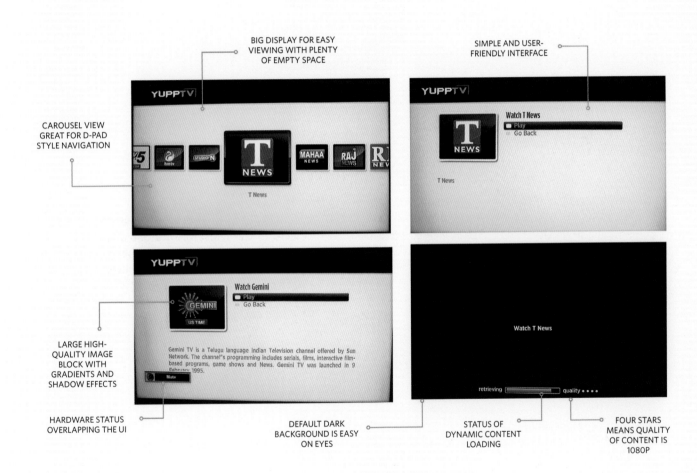

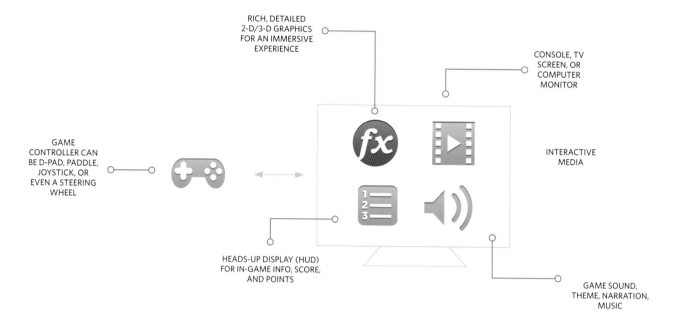

RICH, DETAILED 2-D/3-D GRAPHICS FOR AN IMMERSIVE EXPERIENCE

CONSOLE, TV SCREEN, OR COMPUTER MONITOR

GAME CONTROLLER CAN BE D-PAD, PADDLE, JOYSTICK, OR EVEN A STEERING WHEEL

INTERACTIVE MEDIA

HEADS-UP DISPLAY (HUD) FOR IN-GAME INFO, SCORE, AND POINTS

GAME SOUND, THEME, NARRATION, MUSIC

A console game is an interactive, multimedia-rich, video game application, normally played on high-definition televisions with large screens. It strives for a cinema quality with detailed graphics and features refined storytelling techniques for an immersive experience, which draws a player into a rich and complex game world. The user plays on the screen using a joystick or a wireless controller.

Best Practices and Design Guidelines

- Have action interface mapped with the controller buttons and sensors
- Use heads up display (HUD) for in-game information
- Have multiple feedback systems using graphics, audio, and vibrations
- Have third-person interface to create an illusion of peripheral vision and movielike experience
- Create controller-based actions and prefer D-pad navigation
- Use advanced sound effects for narration, game theme, sound, and music

User Experience

- Use minimum textual information and use standard visual icons
- Use high-quality graphics and fast 3-D rendering
- Have typography match the game theme
- Use bright colors and responsive UI elements
- Have multiple views for the game: God view, camera view, and player view

(+) See also **10-Foot User Interface** on page 182 and **Mobile Game App** on page 144.

Angry Birds Roku TV Version

Angry Birds is a popular console game with rich graphics and a great interactive experience. It uses the Roku player's customized remote as a controller and other game commands.

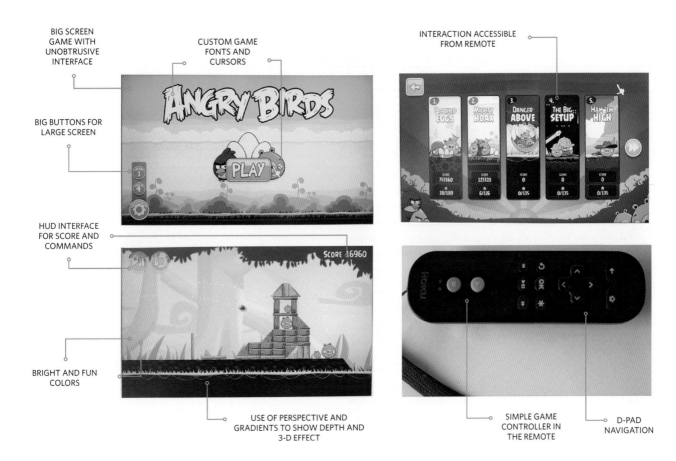

BIG SCREEN GAME WITH UNOBTRUSIVE INTERFACE

CUSTOM GAME FONTS AND CURSORS

INTERACTION ACCESSIBLE FROM REMOTE

BIG BUTTONS FOR LARGE SCREEN

HUD INTERFACE FOR SCORE AND COMMANDS

Score 86960

BRIGHT AND FUN COLORS

USE OF PERSPECTIVE AND GRADIENTS TO SHOW DEPTH AND 3-D EFFECT

SIMPLE GAME CONTROLLER IN THE REMOTE

D-PAD NAVIGATION

93

Welcome Email

THE FIRST EMAIL SENT TO A SUBSCRIBER

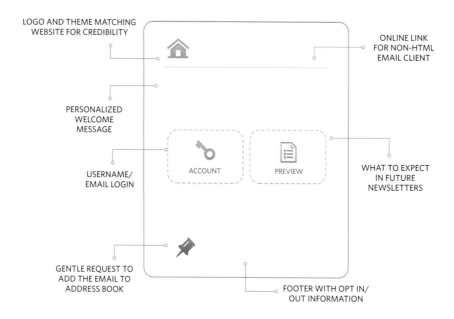

LOGO AND THEME MATCHING
WEBSITE FOR CREDIBILITY

ONLINE LINK
FOR NON-HTML
EMAIL CLIENT

PERSONALIZED
WELCOME
MESSAGE

ACCOUNT

PREVIEW

USERNAME/
EMAIL LOGIN

WHAT TO EXPECT
IN FUTURE
NEWSLETTERS

GENTLE REQUEST TO
ADD THE EMAIL TO
ADDRESS BOOK

FOOTER WITH OPT IN/
OUT INFORMATION

A welcome email confirms a subscriber to an online service. The service can be a free subscription to discounts, coupons, articles, or paid services such as website hosting or e-zines. The welcome email is the starting point of an opted-in communication and gives a preview of coming newsletters.

Best Practices and Design Guidelines
- Welcome the subscriber with login information
- Use HTML-rich formatting for good design with a minimum of images
- Keep it CAN-SPAM compliant
    - Clearly identified sender with name
    - Relevant subject line (check for spam words)
    - A method for opting out (unsubscribe option)
    - Clear intention and content
    - Valid physical address
- Have link to account information, support, and privacy policy

User Experience
- Keep the welcome email one page long, preferably in one column
- Help users/first-time subscribers get started with the service
- Request to add email address to safe sender list
- Avoid banner ads and special promotions
- Use color and font formatting to create distinguishable blocks of information

(+) See also **Email Marketing Campaign** on page 188 and **Email Newsletter** on page 190.

MailChimp.com Welcome Email

MailChimp.com provides an online service for email marketing. It uses a single-column layout for content, with rounded corners. The design uses rich HTML with only two graphical images for the logo and the mascot, which adds credibility to the email.

ONE-PAGE RICH
HTML WITH
MINIMAL GRAPHICS

LOGO ADDS
CREDIBILITY

START HERE
BUTTON

CYAN
BACKGROUND
WITH LOTS OF
WHITE SPACE FOR
AESTHETIC LOOK

ACCOUNT
INFORMATION

STARTER
INFORMATION

QUICK LINKS
TO BLOG AND
KNOWLEDGEBASE

PHYSICAL
ADDRESS

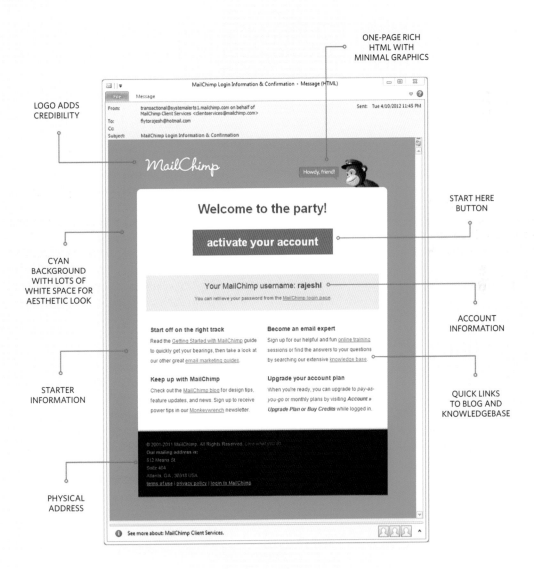

94

Email Marketing Campaign

AN EMAIL PROMOTING A PRODUCT, A SERVICE, OR AN EVENT

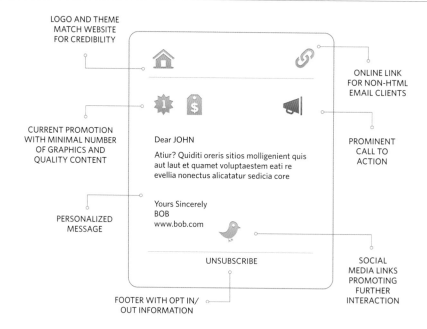

LOGO AND THEME MATCH WEBSITE FOR CREDIBILITY

ONLINE LINK FOR NON-HTML EMAIL CLIENTS

CURRENT PROMOTION WITH MINIMAL NUMBER OF GRAPHICS AND QUALITY CONTENT

PROMINENT CALL TO ACTION

Dear JOHN

Atiur? Quiditi oreris sitios molligenient quis aut laut et quamet voluptaestem eati re evellia nonectus alicatatur sedicia core

Yours Sincerely
BOB
www.bob.com

PERSONALIZED MESSAGE

UNSUBSCRIBE

SOCIAL MEDIA LINKS PROMOTING FURTHER INTERACTION

FOOTER WITH OPT IN/ OUT INFORMATION

An email marketing campaign is the process of sending emails to a large group of people with promotional ads to sell products or services. It is an individual marketing message sent for a specific purpose and contains an electronic flyer of the current promotion. The email is targeted to subscribers/existing customers as well as potentially new customers who have opted in for the promotion.

Best Practices and Design Guidelines

- Use an HTML table with little inline CSS for the layout
- Use one-column fluid layout, for fixed width, with no more than 600 pixels
- Use a strong subject line with something definitive—avoid selling
- Provide a link for non-HTML email clients and include an unsubscribe option

User Experience

- Keep the email low on images with short paragraphs
- Make your message clear and easy to read
- Use font formatting and table background colors to add richness to the content
- Keep important message at the top for preview pane of email client to 500 pixels
- Avoid video, Flash, and animated GIFs

(+) See also **Homepage** on page 54 and **Email Newsletter** on page 190.

A Book Apart Email Campaign

The email campaign of A Book Apart is aesthetic and focused. The campaign is targeted to designers with two current promotional books. It includes a clear website URL, a physical address, and an unsubscribe option at the bottom of the toolbar.

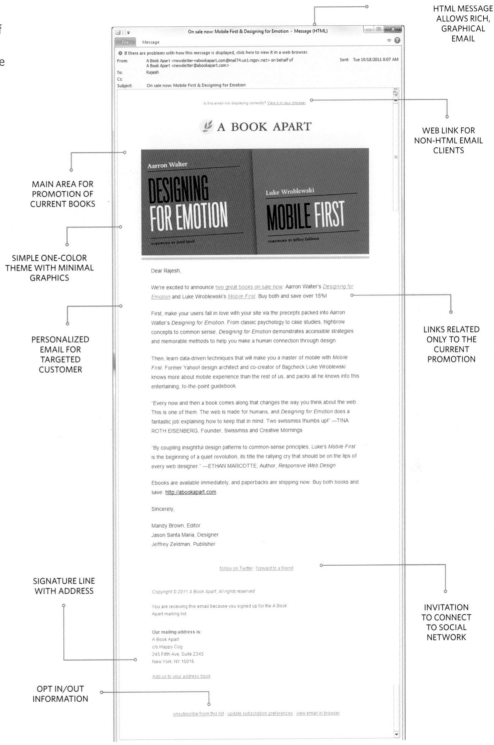

HTML MESSAGE ALLOWS RICH, GRAPHICAL EMAIL

WEB LINK FOR NON-HTML EMAIL CLIENTS

MAIN AREA FOR PROMOTION OF CURRENT BOOKS

SIMPLE ONE-COLOR THEME WITH MINIMAL GRAPHICS

LINKS RELATED ONLY TO THE CURRENT PROMOTION

PERSONALIZED EMAIL FOR TARGETED CUSTOMER

SIGNATURE LINE WITH ADDRESS

INVITATION TO CONNECT TO SOCIAL NETWORK

OPT IN/OUT INFORMATION

95

Email Newsletter

A PERIODIC EMAIL SENT TO SUBSCRIBERS WITH INTERESTING AND NEWSWORTHY CONTENT

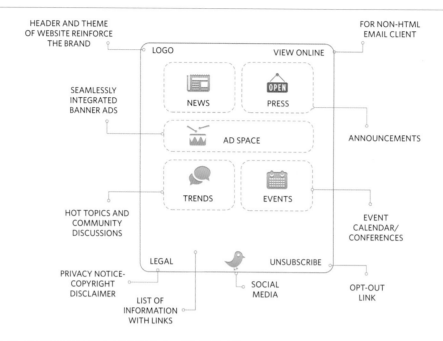

An email newsletter allows online entities to send announcements, press releases, news of events, product launches, and other promotions to customers on a continual basis using email. It helps maintain a relationship with existing subscribers, focuses on brand awareness, and drives website traffic.

Best Practices and Design Guidelines

- Emphasize company brand and use consistent colors from website
- Have one-page, rich email with blocks of information
- Keep it visually engaging with minimal number of optimized images
- For a long newsletter, use a table of contents with anchors
- Keep space for banner ads and affiliate marketing
- Have links to view online, unsubscribe, and see privacy policy and copyright information

User Experience

- Keep the e-newsletter under 100K in size
- Use an HTML table for layout with white space on both sides
- Use headers and titles for easy skimming
- Minimize use of special characters that may not display properly
- Include full URL; if possible, shorten the URL
- Avoid background color, images, and advanced CSS styles

(+) See also **Email Marketing Campaign** on page 188 and **Welcome Email** on page 186.

American College of Radiology Newsletter

The American College of Radiology newsletter theme is simple with a white background. It uses multiple blocks of formatted content with few images, and uses font formatting and color to separate blocks of data.

VIEW ONLINE OPTION

LOGO AND DESIGN FOR BRAND BUILDING

WHITE SPACE WITH WIDE BORDER GIVES DEFINITE STRUCTURE TO THE NEWSLETTER

BLOCKS OF FORMATTED INFORMATION WITH MINIMAL GRAPHICS

COLORED FONTS FOR HEADER AND EASILY DISTINGUISHABLE BLOCKS

GOOD CONTRAST WITH WHITE BACKGROUND AND ACCESSIBLE TEXT

PHYSICAL ADDRESS PER CAN-SPAM REGULATIONS

SOCIAL SHARING OPTION

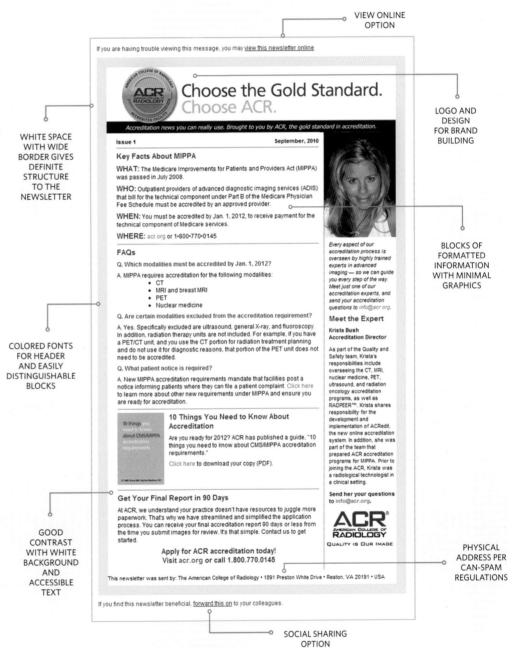

If you are having trouble viewing this message, you may view this newsletter online

Choose the Gold Standard.
Choose ACR.

Accreditation news you can really use. Brought to you by ACR, the gold standard in accreditation.

Issue 1   **September, 2010**

Key Facts About MIPPA

WHAT: The Medicare Improvements for Patients and Providers Act (MIPPA) was passed in July 2008.

WHO: Outpatient providers of advanced diagnostic imaging services (ADIS) that bill for the technical component under Part B of the Medicare Physician Fee Schedule must be accredited by an approved provider.

WHEN: You must be accredited by Jan. 1, 2012, to receive payment for the technical component of Medicare services.

WHERE: acr.org or 1•800•770•0145

FAQs

Q. Which modalities must be accredited by Jan. 1, 2012?

A. MIPPA requires accreditation for the following modalities:
- CT
- MRI and breast MRI
- PET
- Nuclear medicine

Q. Are certain modalities excluded from the accreditation requirement?

A. Yes. Specifically excluded are ultrasound, general X-ray, and fluoroscopy. In addition, radiation therapy units are not included. For example, if you have a PET/CT unit, and you use the CT portion for radiation treatment planning and do not use it for diagnostic reasons, that portion of the PET unit does not need to be accredited.

Q. What patient notice is required?

A. New MIPPA accreditation requirements mandate that facilities post a notice informing patients where they can file a patient complaint. Click here to learn more about other new requirements under MIPPA and ensure you are ready for accreditation.

10 Things You Need to Know About Accreditation

Are you ready for 2012? ACR has published a guide, "10 things you need to know about CMS/MIPPA accreditation requirements."

Click here to download your copy (PDF).

Get Your Final Report in 90 Days

At ACR, we understand your practice doesn't have resources to juggle more paperwork. That's why we have streamlined and simplified the application process. You can receive your final accreditation report 90 days or less from the time you submit images for review. It's that simple. Contact us to get started.

Apply for ACR accreditation today!
Visit acr.org or call 1.800.770.0145

Every aspect of our accreditation process is overseen by highly trained experts in advanced imaging — so we can guide you every step of the way. Meet just one of our accreditation experts, and send your accreditation questions to info@acr.org.

Meet the Expert

Krista Bush
Accreditation Director

As part of the Quality and Safety team, Krista's responsibilities include overseeing the CT, MRI, nuclear medicine, PET, ultrasound, and radiation oncology accreditation programs, as well as RADPEER™. Krista shares responsibility for the development and implementation of ACRedit, the new online accreditation system. In addition, she was part of the team that prepared ACR accreditation programs for MIPPA. Prior to joining the ACR, Krista was a radiological technologist in a clinical setting.

Send her your questions to info@acr.org.

ACR®
AMERICAN COLLEGE OF RADIOLOGY
QUALITY IS OUR IMAGE

This newsletter was sent by: The American College of Radiology • 1891 Preston White Drive • Reston, VA 20191 • USA

If you find this newsletter beneficial, forward this on to your colleagues.

96

E-zine

A MINI ELECTRONIC MAGAZINE WITH INFORMATIVE ARTICLES SENT TO SUBSCRIBERS ON A REGULAR BASIS

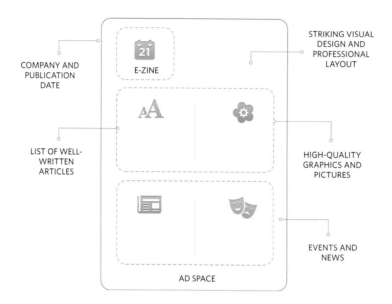

COMPANY AND PUBLICATION DATE

E-ZINE

STRIKING VISUAL DESIGN AND PROFESSIONAL LAYOUT

LIST OF WELL-WRITTEN ARTICLES

HIGH-QUALITY GRAPHICS AND PICTURES

EVENTS AND NEWS

AD SPACE

An e-zine (electronic fanzine) contains well-written articles, helpful information, news, and current trends on a specific topic. It is professionally laid out and edited as an electronic magazine and contains rich graphics and images. E-zines focus on quality original content on a specific topic.

Best Practices and Design Guidelines

- Use clean design and include a table of contents for date of publication
- Use professional graphics for rich look and feel
- Use professional layout for articles with author names and contact information
- Have clear banner ads or space for affiliate marketing
- Keep the email CAN-SPAM compliant and include a privacy statement
- Have a section for upcoming news and events

User Experience

- Focus on quality of the editorial content along with the layout
- Include complete articles
- Keep it a reliable source and publish at the same interval
- Allow the user to print and read offline
- An e-zine is a mini magazine, so keep it between five to ten pages

(+) See also **Email Marketing Campaign** on page 188 and **Email Newsletter** on page 190.

Bellwood Chamber E-zine

This example shows how the Chamber of Commerce of Bellwood Chamber University uses a monthly e-zine to reach out to its subscribers. It has a set of small original articles on current trends and news at the Chamber of Commerce. The layout is very professional with high-quality images.

STRIKING VISUAL DESIGN WITH LOTS OF GRAPHICS

MONTHLY PUBLICATION

RICH LAYOUT WITH HIGH-QUALITY PICTURES

PREMIUM WELL-WRITTEN AND EDITED CONTENT

SET OF SMALL ARTICLES TARGETED TO SUBSCRIBERS

NEWS ABOUT UPCOMING EVENTS

MAGAZINE-STYLE THREE-COLUMN LAYOUT

ADVERTISEMENT SPACE

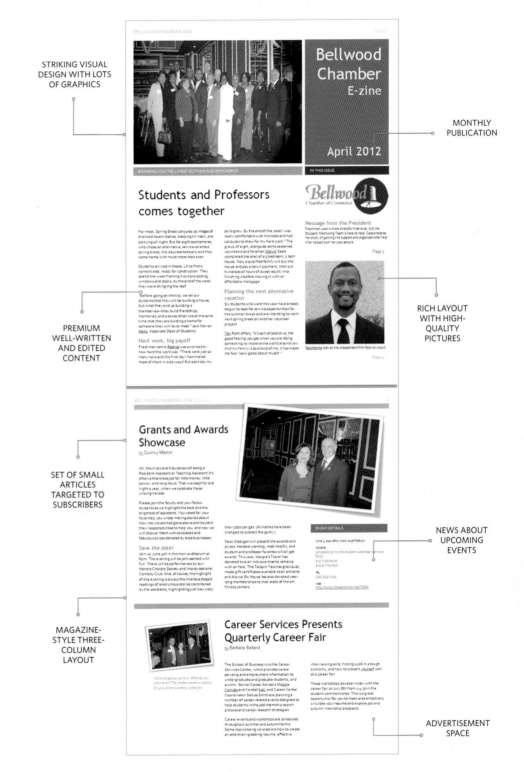

97

Natural User Interface

AN INTERFACE THAT CREATES INTERACTION BASED ON EVERYDAY BEHAVIOR OF USERS

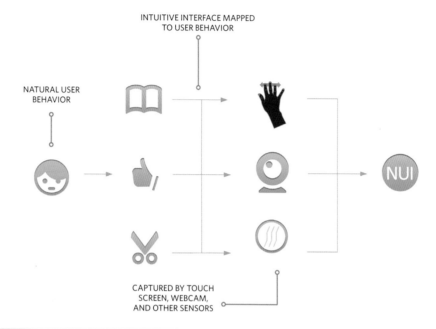

INTUITIVE INTERFACE MAPPED
TO USER BEHAVIOR

NATURAL USER
BEHAVIOR

NUI

CAPTURED BY TOUCH
SCREEN, WEBCAM,
AND OTHER SENSORS

A natural user interface (NUI) is an evolution of the graphical user interface to a more seamless interaction between users and computers. NUI uses natural gestures to interact with applications, as a user would do with a physical object. For example, a gesture to turn a page of a book feels natural on a capacitive screen using multi-touch. NUI can be implemented using touch, gestures, speech, and motion sensors.

Best Practices and Design Guidelines
- Create interface using the natural behavior around the compared physical activity
- Use advanced hardware to map the natural gesture to the interaction
- Allow for learning and self-discovery
- Allow interaction with the content directly
- Keep the interface real time and reactive

User Experience
- Translate key gestures from everyday usage as an interaction
- Have specialized interface based on individual application
- Keep simple and memorable interaction for frequently used items
- Delight user with a seamless and natural interface
- Keep it intuitive and simple

(+) See also **Natural Language Interface** on page 196.

Microsoft Xbox Kinect Sports Game

The Microsoft Xbox Kinect Sports Game console uses a unique remote control to play the game: the user himself. The user stands in front of the console and maps his body to the software. For a table tennis game, the user assumes he has a virtual paddle and plays in front of the console as if he were playing with an opponent. Microsoft Xbox Kinect uses range cameras and voice-processing technologies to track complex movements and gestures that make this possible.

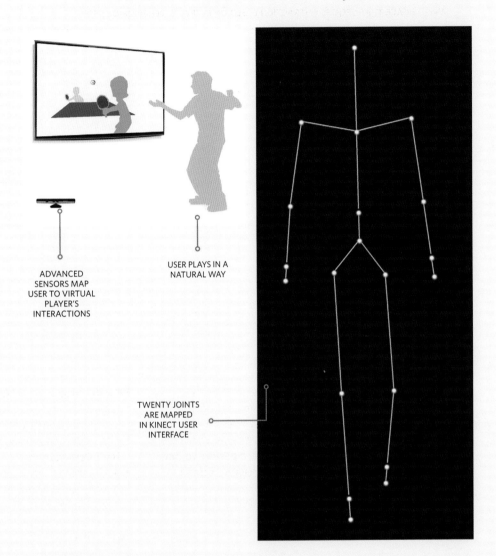

ADVANCED
SENSORS MAP
USER TO VIRTUAL
PLAYER'S
INTERACTIONS

USER PLAYS IN A
NATURAL WAY

TWENTY JOINTS
ARE MAPPED
IN KINECT USER
INTERFACE

195

98

Natural Language Interface

AN INTERFACE THAT USES SPOKEN LANGUAGE TO INTERACT

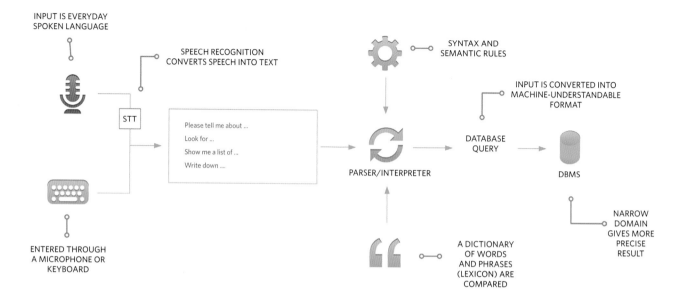

INPUT IS EVERYDAY SPOKEN LANGUAGE

SPEECH RECOGNITION CONVERTS SPEECH INTO TEXT

STT

Please tell me about ...
Look for ...
Show me a list of ...
Write down ....

ENTERED THROUGH A MICROPHONE OR KEYBOARD

SYNTAX AND SEMANTIC RULES

INPUT IS CONVERTED INTO MACHINE-UNDERSTANDABLE FORMAT

DATABASE QUERY

PARSER/INTERPRETER

DBMS

NARROW DOMAIN GIVES MORE PRECISE RESULT

A DICTIONARY OF WORDS AND PHRASES (LEXICON) ARE COMPARED

A natural language interface (NLI) allows a user to interact with a system utilizing a written or spoken language such as English. Everyday phrases, questions, and requests become the commands for the application to query the database. The natural user interface is used in automatic speech recognition (ASR) systems, search applications, dictations, and note-taking applications. NLI works very well when implemented within a specific knowledge domain.

Best Practices and Design Guidelines
- Keep the interface input driven
- Create specialized commands for the application
- Keep ability to teach phonetics, language, and individual style
- Give feedback and show intermediate results
- Give suggested results when no result is retrieved
- Have help screen for most commonly needed phrases and usage

User Experience
- Use vocabulary of that particular knowledge domain
- Filter choices per the context of the application
- Keep an open dialogue interaction between user and computer
- Allow ability to correct a result
- Show progress when processing user query

+ See also **Voice User Interface** on page 180 and **Natural User Interface** on page 194.

Natural Language Interface to FlyEx Database

St. Petersburg State Polytechnical University has created a natural language interface to query its database on fruit flies. The interface allows a user to enter natural language phrases to search for information. It features a quick list of examples to help users formulate their queries.

TAKES A NATURAL LANGUAGE QUERY AS INPUT

ADAPTS TO DIFFERENT METHOD OF FORMULATING QUERY

LIMITS DOMAIN FOR BETTER RESULT

EXAMPLES TO HELP USER

SHOWS INTERMEDIATE QUERY

FLEXIBILITY BY ALLOWING QUERY EDITING

99

Intelligent User Interface

AN INTERFACE THAT LEARNS AND ADAPTS TO USER INTERACTIONS AND COMMUNICATES IN A FRIENDLY, HUMAN WAY

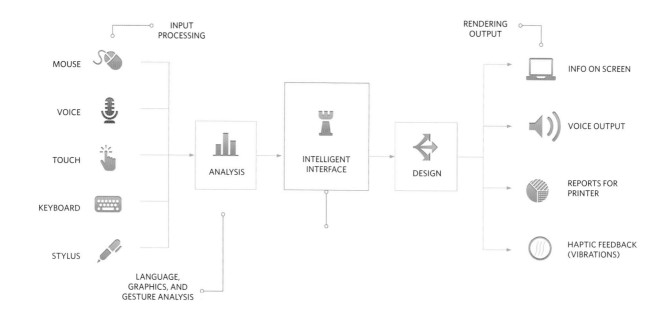

An intelligent user interface allows for a dialogue between the user and the computer. The interface adapts to the user interaction based on the context, maintains knowledge about a user, and interprets and generates natural language utterances, in text or in speech. It maintains a natural language dialogue with the user in combination with other interactions and is also able to explain its results to a user. For example, the famous Boris Electronic Chess Computer saying, "I expected that."

Best Practices and Design Guidelines
- Allow interface to adapt to the interaction for different users and context
- Have integrated user modeling to maintain knowledge about the user
- Integrate natural interface and natural language interface whenever possible
- Allow system to maintain a natural language dialogue with a user
- Keep the design of output rendering intuitive
- Have ability to transparently explain its results to a user

User expectations from an intelligent user interface are a natural feel and an unexpected experience.

User Experience
- Allow for intelligent response if no direct result is found
- Show the intermediate logic for explaining the result
- Have a start screen or quick wizard to help user through the task
- Have a GUI application with access to all items from a keyboard
- Design the interface to help user finish the task

(+) See also **Natural User Interface** on page 194, **Voice User Interface** on page 180, and **Natural Language Interface** on page 196.

Apple iPhone Siri

Apple iPhone's Siri is a virtual assistant that allows for a natural dialogue between the user and the device. Voice input is processed and converted into text and the response is rendered or spoken back by Siri.

SIMPLE UNOBTRUSIVE USER INTERFACE WHICH ACTIVATES ON LONG PRESS OF HOME BUTTON

NATURAL INTERACTION INPUT, VOICE

QUICK HELP ON INTELLIGENT UI USAGE

NATURAL TWO WAY DIALOG WITH THE USER

INTERMEDIATE FEEDWACK TO USER WHILE PROCESSING

RESTRICT RESULTS BASED ON DOMAN 'MOVIES'

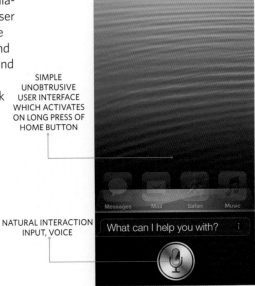

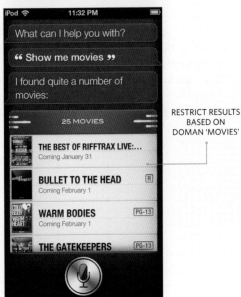

100

Organic User Interface

AN INTERFACE THAT ACCEPTS PHYSICAL OBJECTS AND SHAPES AS INPUT

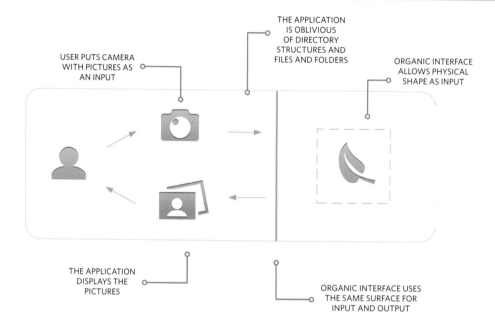

THE APPLICATION IS OBLIVIOUS OF DIRECTORY STRUCTURES AND FILES AND FOLDERS

USER PUTS CAMERA WITH PICTURES AS AN INPUT

ORGANIC INTERFACE ALLOWS PHYSICAL SHAPE AS INPUT

THE APPLICATION DISPLAYS THE PICTURES

ORGANIC INTERFACE USES THE SAME SURFACE FOR INPUT AND OUTPUT

An organic interface takes any object as input and uses the same surface for input as well as output. It utilizes direct manipulations and allows unique interaction techniques with everyday physical objects.

Best Practices and Design Guidelines

- Allow for physical interaction to give a seamless experience with tactile output—for example, an electronic newspaper bending like a real newspaper
- Allow for seamless communication and have multiple interaction points
- Keep a continuous state instead of discrete on and off
- Keep the form of the organic interface fluid and interactive and allow it to change based on the context—unlike GUI, where the screen size and dimensions are fixed

User Experience

- Keep it simple and natural
- Bypass steps to get results
- Avoid computer-like hierarchical structures of menus, folders, and file systems
- Make input of camera object, for example, trigger a photo-importing application and, consequently, photo gallery functionality for displaying the photographs

(+) See also **Natural User Interface** on page 194 and **Natural Language Interface** on page 196.

Microsoft PixelSense App (formerly Microsoft Surface)

Microsoft PixelSense is a unique and interactive surface-computing platform that allows a user to put an object on the surface and interact with it. The table-size screen unifies the input and output on a single surface. It allows for seamless communication with objects and allows recognition of fingers, hands, and objects that are placed on the screen, providing vision-based interaction without the use of cameras.

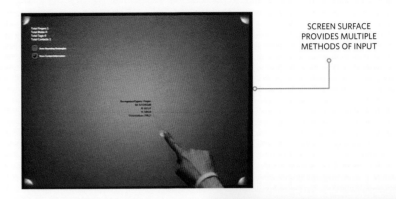

SCREEN SURFACE
PROVIDES MULTIPLE
METHODS OF INPUT

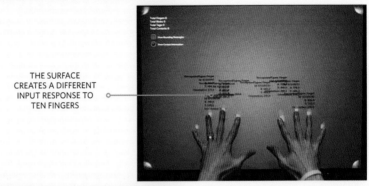

THE SURFACE
CREATES A DIFFERENT
INPUT RESPONSE TO
TEN FINGERS

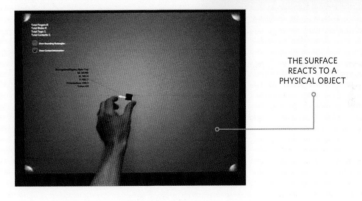

THE SURFACE
REACTS TO A
PHYSICAL OBJECT

Contributors

Andersonwise.com
www.andersonwise.com

Apple
www.apple.com

Bellwood Chamber
www.bellwoodchamber.org

CubeAssembler.com
www.cubeassembler.com

Elegant Themes
www.elegantthemes.com

Freshbooks.com
www.freshbooks.com

Infibeam
www.infibeam.com

Infragistics
www.infragistics,com

Jagriti Sinha
www.jagritisinha.com

Kunal Chowdhury
www.kunal-chowdhury.com

Lakshmi Chaitanya
www.ilakshmi.com

Microsoft
www.microsoft.com

Nokia
www.nokia.com

OliveandMyrtle
www.olivadnmyrtle.com

Paint.Net
www.getpaint.net

Pro Track Online
www.protrackonline.com

QlockTwo
www.qlocktwo.com

Silverlight Fun
www.silverlightfun.com

Survey Monkey
www.surveymonkiey.com

Tastebuds.fm
www.tastebuds.fm

Trulia
www.trulia.com

Voicent
www.voicent.com

Wordpress
www.wordpress.com

Zedo
www.zedo.com

Photo Credits

Anderssonwise.com, 127
Apple Inc., reprinted with permission, 25, 47, 101, 107
Asher Barak, 201
Bellwood Chamber, 193
CubeAssembler.com, 41
ElegentThemes.com, 65
Freshbooks.com, 49
Infibeam, 161
Infragistics.com, 33
Jagriti Sinha, 61
Kunal Chowdhury, 155
Lakshmi Chaitanya, 57
LGPL software, 27
Microsoft, reprinted with permission, 11, 17, 139, 181
Nokia, 157, 165
OliveandMertyle.com, 67

Paint.net, 19
QlockTwo, 135
Shutterstock, 9
Silverlightfun.com, 119
SurveyMonkey, 43
Tastebuds.fm, 179
TrickofMind Gadget, 31,
Trulia, 137
Unicrow.com, 59
University of Washington , Licensed under the Apache License, 13
Vilia, 79
Voicent, 39
W3C, 123
Wikitude, 153
Wordpress , 113
Zedo.com, 55

Acknowledgements

Writing on digital design is like taking on an adventurous journey around the world in eighty days. It is not an easy journey, and it's not for the faint of the heart. There are so many designs to cover and so little time. The world of digital design is ever expanding, and to start at the beginning and cover all the important, current trends in design is a monumental task.

The first thanks goes to William Lidwell, whose book *Universal Principles of Design* (Rockport Publishers 2003) gave me the first inspiration for this book. The book opened my eyes to many exciting design principles that I had never heard of before. I was inspired by his book to the point that I came up with the idea for this book, which takes the same methodology of universal design and applies it on a practical level. It's another book about design principles applied to real digital products: hundreds of email exchanges, tons of designs, and two years of effort later, this book is taking its final shape. Thanks, William.

I also wanted to mention two of the most influential people in the design world who have shaped my thinking on design. One is Steve Jobs, late CEO of Apple, Inc., and the other is Marko Ahtisaari, Nokia design chief. I have learned so much just by listening to them. Thanks, Steve and Marko, for inspiring me.

Thanks to Rita Parada, design technologist at Nokia, who helped me flush out the concept of digital design at the inception of the book. Thanks also to Alex Bravo, my colleague and my friend; an amazing person with whom I had countless discussions on design during last few years, and who knowingly and unknowingly helped me a lot with this book.

Thanks to all the software developers, app developers, and website designers who agreed to include their examples as case studies in the book.

Thanks also to my family, especially Mom, Dad and my brothers, who have always believed in me. Finally, I want to thank my wife Lakshmi, my shining star, for her relentless patience and support during the entire writing period.

About The Author

Raj Lal is an internationally recognized digital product leader who has designed and developed software used by millions of people. He has spent more than a decade designing UIs and has worked on more than fifty desktop, web, and mobile applications. He has also written books on desktop and mobile devices and given presentations on web technologies worldwide. He works at Nokia, in Silicon Valley, as a technologist and lives in Mountain View, California. For more information, please visit http://iRajLal.com. More information on the book can be found at http://dsgnmthd.com. He tweets at @iRajLal

Index